PUTTING IT ALL TOGETHER

is "practical psychological help through a combination of modern techniques and ancient wisdom" (Los Angeles Times) by a "vibrant and eloquent woman of crackling intensity with a fistful of credentials." (San Diego Union) Dr. Irene Kassorla, who has won for herself a solid reputation for group therapy sessions on television in cities all over the country, now helps you help yourself establish better and more satisfying relationships with the people who are important to you.

- **Learn why we create distance between ourselves and the people we want to love us.**
- **Learn how to accentuate the positive to get the best responses from a mate, a child, a friend.**
- **Learn why you married the person you chose and how to cope with the problems inherent in your choice.**
- **Learn how to handle the fear of death that may be keeping you from a close relationship.**
- **Learn how to tell your lover when, how and how much you want in a sexual relationship.**

PUTTING IT ALL TOGETHER

by

Dr. Irene Kassorla

A Warner Communications Company

WARNER BOOKS EDITION

This Warner Books Edition is published by
arrangement with Hawthorn Books, Inc.

Warner Books, Inc., 75 Rockefeller Plaza, New York, N.Y. 10019

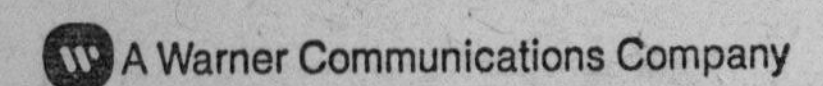

Printed in the United States of America

First Printing: April, 1976

Reissued: December, 1980

10 9

Table of Contents

I want to dedicate this book to my two daughters, Ronnie and Jackie, who have taught me what love means.

Preface

There are so many people who have helped me write this book. It is important for me to affectionately touch them now with my words. I want to express my appreciation.

The beginning of the book started with my girls—Ronnie and Jackie. From the very first day of their lives when they looked up to me, completely helpless, and waited for me to care for them, to feed, caress and love them, I came to understand the meaning of love and dependency. Thank you dear ladies for letting me raise you, for being so precious in my life. Thank you for trusting me.

It was Jackie who put her arms around me when I was in trouble. She knew how to be there, silent, supportive, and helpful. In Chapter XI, when I wrote about warm bodies surrounding the bereaved person, I was thinking how it felt when Jackie hugged me, whenever

I was sad. Her bright mind was able to cut through to what was important in a relationship. I was always in awe of her great sensitivity with people. You know how to caress a person's heart, Jackie.

Ronnie was the one who almost seemed to be able to slip inside my mind, to understand what I was experiencing and to know instinctively where I was emotionally. All was well when she was close by. If there was a problem, she handled it with grace and determination. The range and depth of her ability to feel was beautiful to me. Watching her grow up and develop has been a cherished privilege. Ronnie, I appreciate your great and tender heart—your ability to love.

I am grateful to you and your fiance, Ron Calhoun, for the long hours you both spent helping me edit the book. Your fresh point of view was invaluable to me, and a great gift.

Ron, I enjoyed your excitement at two a.m. when you'd say, "Oh, I love it. This is the best chapter yet. This is really good." You two have helped me to understand the meaning of giving and loving.

Mary Murphy started me writing the book. By reading hours of my philosophy, lectures, and methods, she was able to structure the chapter outline for the book. This outline encouraged me, although I was filled with fear and anxiety, to start the actual writing. Thank you, Mary. I loved our breakfast meetings together, talking and working. I especially enjoyed the feeling of closeness we shared, when occasionally one of my tapes would move us both to tears.

Richard Warren Lewis did the first edit. While I never met Richard, I was on intimate terms with his brown slash marks on the manuscript. He'd write "No!—explain—too brief—out—too colloquial—slang —etc." Richard, I've never seen your face but I know your clever mind, your great wit and skill. Thank you.

I want to thank George Barrie, the President of Fabergé and Brut Productions for his dynamic, innovative approach to television. It was he who approved the purchase of an unknown series, "The Doctor Irene Kassorla Show," from KNXT in Los Angeles. The programs were first shown locally in Southern California. It is the Fabergé company, through its entertainment subsidiary Brut Productions, that is syndicating my TV programs. I appreciate the courage of the Fabergé organization and their willingness to pioneer a new concept on television and bring group therapy into millions of homes.

If a book can have a father, Dan Goodman, the Executive Vice-President of Brut Productions, is "Daddy." It was Dan who first discovered my programs and wanted to syndicate them nationally. Dan's brilliant counsel, sympathy and active help in editing, pulled me through the "rough" days of the book.

My frequent long distance conversations with him were filled with my sometimes tearful worries over pressures and deadlines. Dan consoled and encouraged me. His quick mind always had the solution, while his tenderness assuaged my fears. If I had to pick a father in this world, Dan, it would be you. I am grateful for our association. Thank you.

Gary Mehlman was Dan Goodman's assistant in New York. It was Gary who first reviewed all my television programs. This took weeks of work. He capsulated and wrote a synopsis for each show. I was very touched when Gary sent me a note from New York explaining how much the programs meant to him personally. I was especially pleased when his wife, Karen, told me, "He'd come home every evening filled with Dr. Kassorla and we'd talk during the night about the various shows. The programs brought us closer together."

Gary was eventually transferred to Los Angeles to work with the motion picture division of Brut Productions. It was lucky for me to have him so close by and to be able to call and ask for his help. His prep school training provided him with great expertise in grammar, which led to many fights over those bloody "commas, dangling participles and split infinitives" during the many days we spent editing the book. His voice reading the manuscript brought it to life and made it sound so good. Knowing he would be there until the book was finished gave me a great feeling of confidence. It was fun, Gary, realizing you felt the same way I did about Dan Goodman being "Daddy." I think this means we automatically become brother and sister! I like that.

I'd like to throw kisses to my secretaries Gloria Trossen, Linda Cooper, and Barbara Kadish for all their help and affection.

I want to thank Beverlee Ison for the final edit. I enjoyed your professionalism and your great warmth, Bev. You made me feel the book was precious. Thank you.

I would like the Editors to know how much I appreciated their assistance. I understand I've broken many literary rules. My message in this book is often spoken rather than written. What I've wanted most was to translate the emotional music of my messages to you, the reader.

I have a feeling you will understand that I've wanted to be with you, to touch you with my words—in my own way.

I'm almost sad to be finished now. I've felt good abut ME writing these words to share with YOU. It filled my life, my thoughts, my days and my nights. It is my hope that this book will bring more joy and tenderness into your life. I hope you will be able to move closer to the people you love.

Chapter I

Distance

This is a book for lovers and people who want to fall in love with their friends, their children, their work and themselves.

I find that most patients' ability to fall in love and stay in love is limited by a phenomenon called distance. By distance, I mean that we all find it uncomfortable and frightening to come too close to each other emotionally, so we learn ways to separate and stay apart.

Everybody surrounds themselves with a certain amount of physical and emotional space and cannot allow anyone to intrude on that space for any length of time. When we feel that we are getting too close, we find ways to separate—to stop the love and pleasure in our lives, and to subconsciously sabotage the "intimate moment."

This idea of needing space was demonstrated to me by a new patient this week. She came in to see me because she was worried about her "after sex" behavior with her husband. She explained, "I don't understand—the minute we're finished making love I feel so nervous, I need to jump out of bed and empty the dishwasher or something else just as silly. Why Doctor?"

"I'm not certain," I said. "I'll need to know more about you. What you're experiencing is very common. Most of my patients report that they rush away from each other after making love. They tell me they start cleaning the oven, raiding the refrigerator, taking out the trash, fighting and moving away—anything so they can separate and stop experiencing the pleasure. We all need to create distance, and we find many ways to do this. You'll learn in our work together why it is so frightening to feel too good, to get too close, and why we unconsciously try to sabotage our beautiful moments."

We are all mortal, vulnerable and fragile human beings. No one can give us any assurances about any of us being alive, or in love tomorrow. All we have is the moment we are experiencing now. I call this the *precious moment*. It is so critical to taste it, enjoy it and live it with yourself and the people you love.

We spend much of our lives playing out unhealthy, self-destructive ways to create distance. We stop the love feelings so that when our loves do leave, either by death or by falling in love with someone else, we won't feel the hurt. We'll survive.

To avoid this ultimate hurt and rejection, we maintain our distance from the people we love. We are terrified to get too close.

A relationship that is too close is frightening, even for people who have been married for many years. Being committed to one person in an age when relationships are becoming so disposable, feels too unsafe; we become frightened of being abandoned. We need distance from the people we love the most, and unconsciously, we create it.

We establish this distance in many ways. Each couple finds a method of separating. Some move away from each other through meaningless arguments or extra-marital affairs. Other couples destroy their *precious moments* by bringing up problems about their children or work at the very moment when they are feeling the closest. With other partners, distance is created by battling over money, jealousy, in-laws, child-rearing practices, sex, or the lack of it. These battles work to keep the distance.

The underlying core of most of the problems I've encountered with my patients, whether I treated them in the Far East, Europe or the United States, is that we are all unconsciously motivated to avoid the pain of feeling rejection when the person we love leaves us. As children, we are concerned about our parents rejecting us; as adults, our focus expands to the many people in our intimate worlds who might reject us.

We often hear people say the chemistry in their relationship is sensational. What they are really saying is that the distance they unconsciously agree to stay apart from each other, is mutually comfortable, even though it may be painful.

Our mothers and their mothers before them taught us how to set up what I refer to as "emotional boundaries" or "emotional distancing."

By emotional boundaries or emotional distancing I mean each family has a style for expressing feelings such as anxiety, anger, fear, love, joy, guilt and sorrow. In order to survive, the child must learn to behave emotionally in a way that is acceptable to his parents.

For example: if the child is frustrated and becomes furious, he must express his fury in the family style. He wouldn't be allowed to say to his mother, "I could kill you! I wish you were dead for not giving me that cookie!" This is not the acceptable family formula for anger. He must use the family recipe for anger which may include whining, crying, stomach aches, temper tantrums or whatever.

We also learn from our mother, a woman with beautiful intentions, how to establish our limits for closeness. In this book, when I say "mother," it is really a symbolic term I use to include mother/father/grandparents and each former generation who learned and passed on the family method of interacting with the child.

For each family, these emotional boundaries determine precisely what feelings are allowed to surface and come "out of our mouths." As children, we are trained to deal with our anger indirectly. Few of us have learned how to get our angry words DIRECTLY out of our mouths. We are forced to rely on our family patterns of dealing with this anger which may be self-destructive to our bodies, our love relationships or careers. One of the goals of therapy is to help the patient become aware of his angry feelings, and to express them verbally. Most of us submerge our anger and use substitute vehicles we learned from our families. The healthy ideal is to get our feelings into words and directly out of our mouths!

Each of us attempts to find a partner with the same family training in terms of emotional distancing. Subconsciously, we understand and experience this concept on our very first date.

For example, if I'm from Family A and can tolerate only 10% affection, and you're from Family B and need to give 40% affection, I'll find you suffocating as a lover. We'll probably be incompatible.

Precise emotional matching needs to occur on Date #1. I'll need to find a 10%-er. You'll look for a 40%-er.

If your family styles are similar to mine, we'll probably feel comfortable. We will look attractive to each other.

Typically, the anxiety level is very high on the first date. Both partners are nervous. Neither will talk about feelings; our family styles don't allow this. Each one is afraid to be too direct or share openly.

In order to reduce first date fear feelings, we utilize anxiety reducers instead of saying directly how frightened we are. Perhaps we drink too much; liquor will work as an anxiety-reducer.

Neither one of us has had any early training in sharing frightening feelings. We were not allowed to express fear. We've been trained to use alternative behaviors instead. If our emotional alternative-styles match, and if our family percentages for getting close match, then "it works" and we'll go out another time.

If my family style is too different from yours, it will be uncomfortable for us to be together. Our emotional gears won't mesh. We'll each use some kind of rationalization: I'll say to myself, "I don't like the way his breath smells," and he'll say to himself, "She's too fat." If we match, I'll say, "I love his personality, his looks, his interest in music—he's wonderful, etc." If we mismatch, we'll probably never see each other again and will unconsciously conclude we didn't like the others' politics or manners and remain unaware of the deeper meaning for the split. We won't realize the reason we didn't like each other was because our emotional styles of distancing and getting close were too different.

Your emotional computers must get to work in terms of psychological meshing, or you don't get together for Date #2!

The point is that distance has to be maintained as set down in our childhood by our individual family styles. No one risks coming really close for very long. It's important to be able to look at and understand the way *you* create distance.

Most couples have a hook which they use throughout a relationship in order to stay apart and maintain their emotional distance. I overeat/You over-drink. I lose too much playing cards/You've wiped out our savings on the stock market. I come home tired and depressed about business problems/You nag and complain about your awful day with the kids. I overcharge in the stores/You forget to pay the bills. I take diet pills/You take sleeping pills. I overwork/You have no time for me—only for your charities and the children. I work days/You work nights.

When we are getting too close during a lovely, intimate dinner, I mention our son's bad grades and the *precious moment* stops. That way, one of us can pull back from the other and feel safer—BECAUSE GETTING REALLY CLOSE IS SO FRIGHTENING.

The major reason we are so terrified of putting all our love into another human being, is that we realize we are mortal. *No one is getting out of this life alive.* We are stuck with this reality, although few people think about or experience this fear consciously. So—how can you dare love anybody when you know that person is going to die, and ultimately you're going to be wiped out, left alone, deserted! Even if your mate doesn't die for forty years, the relationship may die sooner. So you stay away because of your fear of becoming dependent on someone else's love.

You say to yourself, "I'm afraid if I only love one person, he could leave me. If he does, I'll be finished. I'll die inside. So if I keep an appropriate distance or have someone else on the side, I'll be safe. Then if he leaves me—for any reason—I won't fall apart."

All we have is the *precious moment*. When your love leaves, whether by death or someone else taking him away, the end is the same. We mourn. So take the moment. Live it. Feel it with your lover, your child, your friend.

This book really started in 1962, in Los Angeles, when I first came in contact with psychotic (seriously emotionally disturbed) children in a hospital setting. I observed the children playing and interacting with their teachers, using the strangest, most pathetic life styles I have ever seen. Sometimes as I watched them scream, scratch, cry and injure their own little bodies, I had the fantasy that I was watching animals manipulate their environments to get what they needed.

When a psychotic child wanted attention, he'd bang his head against the wall and the nurse would run over and rock him; when he wanted a hug, he'd jab a scissors into his cheek. He wasn't able to say "I want" in a normal way. But the bizarre behavior worked. The child got what he wanted—the nurse hugging him.

The behavior of these children was so obvious, it was easy to see the transaction:

Do something sick → get hugs and affection.

My practice with psychotic adults started in 1966, in London. My first patient hadn't talked or moved much for thirty years. Desperately rejected in a love affair, he unconsciously decided that if he remained silent and immobilized, no one could hurt him any more.

The child who injured his body did get attention and affection. The British man who went dead for 30 years did avoid further rejection.(1) Psychotic behavior does work; the problem is the cost; it is staggering in terms of human suffering and wasted lives.

It was in London that I first started seeing normal patients, and the parallels between psychotic and normal behavior became apparent to me even though they were very subtle.

My normal patients, like the psychotics, didn't seem to have direct words or the ability to express themselves *out-of-their-mouths*. They were not able to communicate their needs: how they hurt, how lonely they were, how much they wanted to love and to be loved. They couldn't share their feelings. Rather, they used roundabout strategies and devious tactics. Their behavior wasn't sick; they were just sad. Their indirect methods of communication created undue loneliness and misunderstanding in their lives.

(1) Kassorla, Irene C., *The Modification of Verbal Behavior by Operant Conditioning in Chronic Schizophrenia: an Experimental Single-Case Study*. Senate House, University of London, June, 1968.

I have found this identical inability to communicate feelings in patients I've seen all over the world. We're all the same. We're all really afraid to open up with our feelings and say what we need; we're too afraid to be hurt or rejected. We are all vulnerable!

Our emotional life-styles are established as very small children when we have little understanding of the importance of life and loving. None of us would consider asking a small child about world affairs or business problems. Yet, as adults, we continue to rely on the frail and immature emotional foundations we pieced together in our childhoods; we conduct our lives today using the ideas and values we formulated in our earliest years. It makes more sense to design your adult life-style with your 20, 30 or 80 year old eyes and experience.

How do we change old, established patterns? Is it possible? My work demonstrates change is *very* possible. If you had sufficient intelligence as a small child to learn your family's old emotional patterns, then you can learn new modes of behavior. If we can learn to understand how we create distance, because of our childhood fears and problems, we will be able to stop our "distancing," and come closer to the people we love.

I want to share with you the experiences I've had in working with my patients in order to help you see the methods we all use to create distance and unwittingly destroy our lives. There are alternative behaviors that are available to you. There are healthier and happier ways for you to increase your choices and expand your life-styles.

Chapter II

How We Create Distance

I've treated patients in many parts of the world—Europe, the Middle East, the Far East, North Africa and South America. I've observed family interactions on a sampan in Aberdeen, near Hong Kong, and I've treated a titled family in a mansion in Rome. These people were very much the same; they were all too frightened to get close.

It is not only the rare person or the cold person who has these fears—nor is this fear unusual or unique. *Everyone* is afraid to get too close! Everyone learns his own way to create "Distance." I have never met a person or couple who could get very close emotionally.

We learn how much closeness is allowed and how much distance is tolerated from our parents, as they do from their parents, grandparents and back through time. When we were small and hugging and kissing mother, she may have stopped us at a certain point. If we jumped onto her lap and she had already reached her tolerance level of closeness (say we had wanted 45% closeness, when mother could only stand 30%), then mother would push us away, explaining, "Oh, I have to make a roast now, or I have to call Grandma, or I have to scrub the bathroom floor." We learn our tolerance for closeness from our mother. It is her emotional style that becomes fixed in our personality patterns.

As adults, we typically go out and marry someone like our mother. Both the male and the female find their mother-types. We all look for the person who, like ourselves, has the same happiness limits, as well as the same style for dealing with guilt, anxiety, fear and other emotional pain.

Each couple has a "fight shelf" they can refer to when things are going too well. We have a little storage place hidden in our subconscious where we file away angry memories. When we are dealing with our lovers, and we've reached our tolerance for closeness, one partner can pull something out from the fight shelf. This guarantees an argument or an ending of the *precious moment*. It re-establishes the emotional distancing we've rigidly set up from our childhoods. Like the mother who ended the close *precious moment* by running to her roast, we end this same moment by grabbing some old grievance from the past to start a fight and to stop the pleasure.

Each couple plays out "stopping the pleasure" in their own style. And while the styles are different, the basic theme of maintaining distance seems to be the same. As you read the following vignettes, you'll probably identify with the individuals and see yourself in some of them—which may demonstrate that you're not only willing to cry or laugh at yourself a bit, but also willing to look at some of the dynamics of your own relationships. You may find your mate in some of them. You'll see your friends; Aunt Tillie will be there too, and of course, yourself. If you are willing to *look at yourself*, change is possible.

Each example is a composite of patients I've treated in various parts of the world. None of them are real people as stated, but, the pain and suffering that distance created in their lives is shared by all of us.

HEAVENLY WEEKEND—MISERABLE MONDAY

Howard and Carol came to me when they were on the verge of a divorce. They both felt the marriage was hopeless but they wanted to give it one last try—one last "shot" with Dr. Kassorla.

Howard grumbled that Carol was . . . "a dried up bitch. She never gives me any love or affection. In fact, I haven't seen her nude in weeks."

"He never leaves me alone for a minute," Carol complained. "Every time I look up, he's standing there wanting to make love, ready to pounce on me. We're always fighting about sex or the children or something. There's just no peace in our house."

After a few sessions, they reported to me that they had enjoyed a beautiful, intimate weekend. They felt so good about each other. It was dear and close and sensual; by Sunday they were both ecstatic. At breakfast on Monday, one of their small daughters, Howard's favorite, spilled her milk. Carol loudly scolded the four-year-old child. Howard interrupted suggesting, "It's not such a big deal—just a little spilled milk." Carol turned on him and started screaming; she was tired of being the maid and always cleaning up the messes after him and the children.

Howard explained to me later that he couldn't believe that the cold deadly face of this "vicious, yelling harpy" was the woman he had loved so tenderly for the past three days. He was wounded, hurt and furious. The closeness of their intimate time together was *instantly over.*

I felt that the ecstasy of the weekend was too frightening for both of them. Carol stopped it by picking on their daughter, which she knew (unconsciously) would disturb Howard and draw him into an argument with her.

If Carol had not stopped the *precious moment*, I believe Howard would have. Even though he complained about her frigidity and coldness, he was as much afraid of their intimacy as she was.

It's as though there's an unconscious agreement between couples—a pact lovers make: "Darling, if we breach our emotional boundaries and get closer than our family styles will allow, remember that one of us has to start a fight. If I fail to remember dear, I hope you will!"

YOU WORK—I'M LONELY

Gregg is a self-made, middle-aged man—the produce king of a large major city. Much of his time is spent working fifteen-hour days away from home. He travels during the week to his suppliers in various parts of the state. Mary, his pretty, blonde and very young wife, complains that work comes first, the children second, and she comes maybe fifth after the dogs and servants. Mary walks around their mansion filled with rare antiques and priceless art, with two swimming pools and a tennis court, feeling lonely, sullen and rejected.

Gregg and Mary need more distance than most couples I treat. This is probably because there was so much neglect and sadness in their childhood. Gregg's mother left him and his father when he was four years old. Once she was gone, she never attempted to see or phone the child again. He always felt unworthy and unloved. He interpreted that, "If your mother leaves you, it is because you are worthless. If I were *good* enough she would have stayed to love me and take care of me."

Mary's childhood, while very different from Gregg's, had many of the same components. Her mother was a depressed personality and spent much of her time alone in her room. Furthermore, she was hospitalized for a psychotic episode for two years when Mary was three and again for another year when Mary was seven. Mary concluded, in her child-like mind, "My mother leaves me all the time because I don't deserve her. I'm bad. If I were a good girl she wouldn't get sick. She would stay home with me."

Both Gregg and Mary lived with too much loneliness and neglect early in their lives. I believe they selected each other because they unconsciously realized that the level of loneliness they established as children could be relived in their marriage. All we have are the tools and skills we learn as children. We bring these skills into our contemporary lives and blindly blame our partners for our loneliness, as Gregg and Mary do.

When Gregg comes home at night, he is full of ambivalent feelings. He's eager to see Mary whom he adores. But he's so uncomfortable hearing her complaints about his "damned work," he hates coming home. She says, "You think more of your lettuce crop than me. I despise your work. We don't need the money. Why can't you think of me and stay home once in a while?" Since they fight most of the time about work, he feels lonely when he's home and he also feels lonely when he is on the road all week. Work is like the "other woman" for Mary. Instead of sharing their pain and loneliness and talking about how much they love and need each other, it's always battle-time. Over the phone, there are some tender moments. They can experience being close verbally if they are far enough removed physically. I believe Mary and Gregg married each other because each unconsciously realized neither could tolerate more than a few minutes of pleasure before one of them would start the distancing with a fight.

Both Gregg and Mary are very negative to each other. Yet Gregg will tell friends what a good mother and how "gorgeous, precious and desirable" Mary is, and how lucky he is. To Mary, he complains and talks about his loneliness, his resentment and how difficult he finds it living with her. The same is true for her. She praises Gregg's thoughtfulness and generosity to her friends but can rarely give him a positive word or an expression of affection when they are together.

Mary and Gregg are in love—but they seldom tell each other. Do you? When was the last time you told your lover: "I need you—I want you—I adore you." *Do it right now*!

PUNISHING MAMA—NAUGHTY LITTLE BOY

Although both partners are approximately the same age, Ann is the good, responsible, wise and sensible mother in the marriage while Hugh is the bad little boy. Ann is a robust, stocky (just a bit chubby) and very pretty Danish woman who is forty-one years old. Sometimes she sounds more like a mother when she talks to Hugh, than a wife.

Hugh is a handsome, trim forty-year old. He's busy flirting with other women wherever he goes. His extramarital behavior is unknown to his wife. Hugh looks about ten years younger than Ann. He's very athletic and rarely misses his five-mile jog along the beach in front of their home.

Ann speaks to her husband (even when she's asking him to pass the salt) in an annoyed, stern, punishing voice as though he were a naughty five-year-old.

Hugh clearly represents the boy in the marriage relationship. He is always doing something naughty, like lying, hiding, or covering up some evidence he doesn't want his mommie-wife, Ann, to find out. He often takes other women to dinner and/or a motel. When he gets home at 4:00 a.m., he tells Ann that he got lost out of town on the road or had a flat tire or had important work to do. Ann believes him and scolds him. Then, of course, she forgives him, and everything is fine.

The bulk of his lying isn't related to extra-marital relationships, however. Hugh is a compulsive gambler. Every chance he gets to leave work or Ann, he's on a quick flight to Las Vegas. He can lose as much as $1,000 shooting craps, while Ann, on the other hand, is always pinching pennies. She will buy herself a $10 dress or take hours at the supermarket scrutinizing labels to determine which can of tomatoes has more ounces for the money and which can of peaches is one-half cent cheaper. She is scrimping while he is out gambling. He's constantly manipulating funds, using mortgage payment money for gambling, then borrowing funds to cover up his losses. He's very clever and is able to get away with these maneuvers by occasional wins. He's always worried about "Momma" Ann finding out, which she frequently does. Then she gets very irate, and they don't talk to each other for a few days. Finally, he is irresistibly charming, abandons gambling for a few weeks, and his transgressions are forgiven. Soon the events are re-cycled. Hugh again starts the gambling and lying; Ann responds with her scolding; their distance is again established.

Ann and Hugh originally came to see me because their 16-year old son had been arrested for drunk driving. After a few sessions, it became apparent that it was the parents who needed the therapy, not their son.

Once Ann and Hugh started working on the problems of their relationship, the son's behavior improved markedly.

Early in their therapy, I suggested that Ann match Hugh's gambling behavior. Every time he lost $1,000 on cards, I suggested she go out and buy $1,000 worth of clothing, jewelry or whatever she wanted. This may seem like a rather bizarre solution, but, in fact, a few months after she started matching his losses, Hugh's lust for gambling seemed to disappear. He became far more sensible when he was confronted with the problem of manipulating $2,000 each time his losses amounted to $1,000.

Why did the gambling stop? For the mama/son (or I'm good/you're bad) pattern to work, each partner has to play out his role. This maintains the distancing. Ann had to be the penny-pinching, nagging mama, and Hugh needed to continue being the frivolous child. When Ann matched Hugh and spent $1,000, there were two children present in the relationship and the mama/son model no longer held. Their unconscious plan for distancing lost its effectiveness.

Once we reached the stage where the symptomatic or defensive behaviors stopped (her scolding, his lying, etc.) we were able to get to work on the underlying problem—their fear of getting close.

DID I MAKE YOU JEALOUS, HONEY?

Burt and Nona play the jealousy game very well. Each of them takes turns dropping stories about their activities during the day which are designed to worry the other. For example, Nona was telling Burt, at the dinner table one evening, about the marvelous afternoon she had at her bridge club. "I had an excellent partner! What a treat it was to be with a master bridge player. And he had such a sense of humor. Honey, I just have to tell you this adorable, lewd and sexy story he told us. You'll roar."

Then Nona goes into painstaking detail about the blue joke making sure she includes every slang term related to genitals and copulating, because, she says slyly, "that's how he told the joke to me!" This triggers all kinds of jealous fantasies for Burt who imagines Nona was going to bed with her bridge partner while he was killing himself at work.

Jealousy is a well-used separator. Often, one partner thinks the other is uninterested in him and uses jealousy as a manipulation. "Maybe if I just drop a little jealousy bomb in his lap, it'll bring him closer to me." The jealousy statement says, "Hey, look at me. Everyone else is interested in me; everyone else loves me; everyone else wants to go to bed with me. You better love me, or I'll leave." Unfortunately, the use of jealousy doesn't work, as the love partners invariably become frightened, less trusting and move *even farther away*. Jealousy doesn't result in closeness, it creates *distance*.

SEX AND BREAKING THE BARRIERS

When you have sex, you literally destroy distance; the bodies interlock and become one. Two bodies facing and caressing are so closely joined, no space can be seen; they appear to be sealed. The locked-in position of sex is the closest two people can get physically. If they are in love, the bond is further enhanced by emotional factors, and the couple move even closer together. This is an exquisite state. Even mechanically, it seems so right—everything fits. Their genitals are connected, their bodies are connected, their mouths are connected, their arms are embracing. This is a beautiful, picturesque kind of closeness.

But we can't stand too much of it!

After sex, so-called reality sets in, and unconsciously we think, "Hey, what have I done? We've completely melded! I've destroyed the barriers. I've dared to get absolutely close." Unconsciously we panic, but we are still conscious enough to act and make sure we move our bodies away from each other. Thereby, we reestablish our distance.

If I can pick up my body and say, "Oh my goodness honey, I've got to take a shower," or "Gee honey, are you hungry? I'm going to get some orange juice," then I can get some physical distance, and we can start later, when we have enough separation, to reconstruct the gap.

The point is, love of mine, I'm too close to you. I'm hearing too many violins. I don't want to get this close. I don't want to feel so exposed. I don't want to feel this dependent, because, what will I do if you should leave me? What do I do when you're gone?

These fears come on so quickly that I have to move fast. I run to the kitchen for food. You go to your cigarette and tell me about your aggravating boss. We'll argue a little bit about what happened at the party last night or about the children.

Thank God! We've re-established our distance!

HOME SWEET PAIN

Sheila says she waits all day for Sean to come home. When she hears his car in the driveway she feels excited. But when Sean turns the doorknob, Sheila starts feeling awful. She doesn't want to get near him. She almost wants to run. She says to herself, "I don't understand. A few minutes ago, I was filled with love. Why, when he walks in the door, should I suddenly want to start fighting? I must be crazy! How could I look forward all day to his coming home—and now that he's here, why do I want to get away from him? There must be something wrong with me!"

Sheila's feelings are normal. Many of my patients, both male and female, have expressed these same feelings. When they occur, I suggest they share with their partners the full message of what they are experiencing. Your partner is probably just as confused.

This is what Sheila was thinking and really wanted to say: "Darling Sean, I'm delighted you are home—but, I'm so mixed up—so hostile and angry. I really love you, but for some reason I don't understand, I want to start a fight. You are the only person in the world for me. There is no one else I want to be with. But when we're not fighting, I become frightened and feel anxious. So please—let's start a fight!"

I asked Sheila how she would feel about telling Sean the thoughts she shared with me. She said, "I would feel crazy saying things to him like, "I love you, let's fight!"

Nevertheless, she had been thinking those thoughts. Sheila was saying nice words to Sean, but they weren't what she was feeling. She didn't understand her anger. As a result, she wanted to stay away from her husband. Then she wouldn't have to experience those "crazy, love/fight feelings."

One of the reasons that these mixed feelings are so common in our adult lives, is that most of us associate a great deal of comfort, safety and good feelings with our childhood homes. However, we also associate this same home with a lot of painful, scary, and awful feelings. This adds up to a package called "home" in our memory, a combination of wonderful/awful, happy/terrible feelings. It was *wonderful* when mother loved and hugged us, but it was so *awful* when she screamed and looked angry.

When we get married, we try to recreate the safe environment we had with mother. But because our childhood memories are also filled with pain and fear, we unconsciously have to put these ingredients in our homes, as well.

People become anxious when there is no emotional pain in the home. They say to themselves, "Something must be missing." They remember childhood and the horrible moments—the nightmares of growing up. So they decide, "Trouble must be coming up any minute." Unconsciously, they make certain that it does.

Both parts of the love-pain connection need to be included in our contemporary lives. Home would be unfamiliar with only love and good feelings. When the new patient begins to realize that he does seek out the love-pain combination in his life, it frightens him. This wonderful/awful concept causes all kinds of confusion and contradiction.

In Sheila's case, because she felt like the "naughty-little girl" in the marriage, it was easy for her to introduce the pain. When Sean came in the door with a big smile Sheila would say "You can't believe what happened today . . . etc." She would then go on to outline her mistakes and delinquent acts. Once Sheila told her story, Sean's smile would vanish. He would look disgusted and begin screaming. This was the typical way their evening began.

If Sheila hadn't done anything "wrong" that day, peace might be maintained until they sat down at the dinner table. Invariably, one of the children would start something. They had also learned the family style!

You *can* change now! It is never too late. Talk this over with your partner. Work together. Share childhood experiences so you can help one another. Say to your lover: "I learned a painful style of living when I was little. Right now, I want to start an argument over nothing in our house. But I know I want to stop repeating my childhood. Put your arms around me and help me get through this without fighting. I need you."

Very few of us have the insight or understanding to communicate this kind of message.

We find it more comfortable to be fighting over something trivial than to experience the anxiety of no fighting. Even more frightening is the anxiety which follows the pure pleasure of closeness.

MRS. SUPER-COOL

Connie is thirty-seven and owns a chain of health spa-beauty parlors. Her husband, Randy, is a doctor, specializing in cardiology. Connie is well educated with an exceptional business sense. She's a very "classy lady" who speaks in such a precise, crisp way that when you are with her, you feel as though your hem is a little crooked or maybe your grammar isn't correct.

Connie can handle anything. She thinks there is something wrong with people who are unable to master any situation or problem.

She came to see me recently as a patient and told me she had been in an accident at one of her spas. After business hours, there was an explosion in the basement causing jars and bottles from the shelves in her office to come crashing down all around her. She had fallen to the floor. Broken glass surrounded her and small pieces of glass were covering her body. No one was there to help her.

Connie was in momentary shock, but soon she recovered. She went to the phone and called her secretary to see about replacing the broken jars. Then she called her babysitter to say she would be late; she didn't mention the accident.

Next, she called a friend, and asked her to come to her office to pick up the dogs in the back seat of her car and take them home. She was worried the explosion had frightened her poodles. She called her lawyer to make sure the insurance policy was intact and spoke to everyone in her usual cool manner.

Connie had just been through an enormous shock, and yet she was telling everyone she was "just fine."

She finally called her husband who was at his office working with a repair man on a plumbing problem. She explained that she would be delayed a few moments because she had to go to the hospital but not to worry. "Everything is under control." She was giving instructions without any emotion as though she were reciting a recipe.

When she came to me, she said, "I am furious that Randy didn't come to the hospital. I'll never forgive him. It's so terrible that I can't find a man who will take care of me. My ex-husband never helped me when I needed it, and now Randy is the same way. It's terrible that no one helps me when I'm in trouble." She wanted to leave him. "Who wants a man like him who isn't there when you need him!"

"Connie, who knew you were in trouble?", I asked her. "You got up off the floor, glass and all, worried about your jars and dogs. You're dialing phones, checking on insurance policies . . . You sounded fine. Who could ever guess you were in trouble? There was no way for Randy to know."

She replied, "It is so humiliating to me. I called Randy and he said his bathroom sink was leaking. There was a lot of damage to the carpeting. He had a plumber, and he couldn't leave then. How could he think of that damned plumbing instead of me?"

I told her that Randy had an emergency on his hands, and that because she came off as Mrs. Cool and Mrs. Everything-Is-Under-Control, he didn't know she needed help.

He probably thought she just went to the hospital as a formality.

If Connie had said something like, "I have glass all over me—I'm terrified—I'm scared to death—I'm shaking! I can't stop hearing that terrible crash!" Randy would have dropped everything. He told me later he had no idea she was even upset.

What Connie is unable to see is that she does not give out the proper information for what she needs. In fact, she is terrified to be cared for. She has to sound like Mrs. Cool all the time. Connie doesn't tell her husband what she wants, or needs!

Like Connie, many of us spend too much of our time feeling lonely and unloved because we can't ask for help.

We create the distance in our lives!

MR. OOM-PA-PA AND MRS. BLAH

Vic is an actor's agent in Beverly Hills. He is a successful, dynamic man with a client list that reads like a "Who's-Who" in the film industry. Janet, his wife, apologetically calls herself "just a housewife." She shops most days for clothing for herself and spends one entire day a week in the beauty parlor. Janet is a college graduate. She majored in music and taught this subject in high school. She quit teaching when she married Vic. She wanted to go back to work, but Vic wanted her to stay home and "look pretty and rested for me. I don't want you to have any outside interests to interfere with our marriage." So while Vic's life is full of interesting people, challenges, stimulating meetings and exciting projects, Janet's outside world is limited to trying on clothes, talking to her hair dresser and being negative about herself. Vic is what I call a Mr. Oom-pa-pa and Janet has put herself into the role of Mrs. Blah.

With this kind of combination, the relationship is unequal: one partner makes the decisions thinking he is "right," and the other partner listens obediently.

Vic often boasts that he and Janet never fight. Of course! He makes all the rules, and Mrs. Dumb-Dumb says yes.

The Mr. (or Mrs.) Oom-pa-pas are great "helpers." They are comfortable when helping other people—but the help *must not be returned.* It might sound like this would be a terrific person to have around, always doing altruistic things for someone else, but when you're with Mr. Helper, you'll probably end up feeling very inadequate.

One of the ways the Mr. Oom-pa-pas can avoid getting help is by correcting and criticizing their partners. For example, Vic will say to Janet, "How come you never help me? It's just awful, I have to do everything myself." Janet thinks, "He's right. I must be a selfish bitch. Something's wrong with me, not helping this wonderful guy." But, if she tries to assist him in any way, he starts correcting her, "That's *not* right—you're impossible—more to the left—not that way—can't you do anything right?" It will take an eclipse of the moon before Janet will dare to help him again—she feels so inadequate! Parents do this with children, and they wonder why they can't get "those lazy kids to do anything" when they correct and punish every gesture the child makes.

The relationship with a Mr. Oom-pa-pa is designed so that closeness is almost impossible. It is difficult to be affectionate and loving when you've just been told, "You can't do anything right."

The Mr. Oom-pa-pas need to be in control all the time. By being on the giving end, control is kept in their hands. In this way, no aid or assistance can be offered without their design.

They are "do-it-yourselfers," and they unconsciously instruct the people around them not to be supportive or affectionate. For example, Vic is usually touching, caressing or handling Janet. He is in control of the interaction; he is the GIVER. His arm will either be around her or over her in some affectionate way whenever they are near each other. He complains, however, that she never touches, fondles or hugs him: "Why are you so cold? How come you never hug me? You know I love to be hugged. Why don't you hug me?" Finally she does come through with a hug and he says "Hmmph!, you call that a hug?" By criticizing her affectionate gesture, he punishes her. It is unlikely she'll try again for a while.

Oom-pa-pa behavior is shaped in early childhood by the loving mother who really feels very small and very inadequate herself. My patients report that much of the time they are terrified of their children, overwhelmed, and have no idea how to handle most problem situations. They feel guilty and are sure that all other parents are capable and have all the answers. NOT TRUE! Most of us raise our children on a trial and error basis with spit and string, prayers and lots of hope.

When the disappointed child comes crying to mother, "Johnny doesn't like me—he isn't inviting me to his party," she isn't sure what to do, or how to help. She can't make Johnny like her son. She's concerned she can't even get her neighbors to like her. She gets Johnny to stop crying and stop feeling. Then she changes the subject and gets him to *rely on himself* and to *take care of himself*. After all, she really feels only two years old emotionally. At least her son is now three and one-half, he'll be fine. "Big boys don't cry—the party isn't worth going to anyway—go wash your face and we'll get some ice-cream." She wanted to help ———she wasn't sure how———she did the best she could.

Unconsciously, he realized that Mommie feels better when he says everything is wonderful. Johnny learned crying doesn't work. He can't get any help from Mommie. He knows he has to give her talk about how capable, knowing and wise he is. So at three and one-half, Mr. Oom-pa-pa is well on his way as Mr. Do-it-Yourself, Mr. Don't-Help-Me, Mr. I-Can-Manage-Alone. Help wasn't available—Mommie was too fragile—he had to learn to take care of himself.

In a healthy marriage, each partner is helpless some of the time and powerful, giving, protective and in control some of the time. Each partner is the baby some of the time and the parent some of the time. The ideal relationship is one where you both give and take something for yourself and where there is a great deal of sharing and consideration traded back and forth.

If you're looking for the totally *strong*, *wise*, *superior* adult, I don't know where you'll find this person. DON'T LOOK! The mature personality is like a color wheel, that is, full of shades of strong/fragile, wise/foolish, stable/irresponsible, successful/failing. This is what I call *human*!

The healthiest relationship is a partnership built with two peers struggling and working together on *their* problems: two independent pillars who are able to stand alone as adults and move together to become interdependent because they need someone to love and adore.(1)

(1) Gibran, Kahil, *The Prophet*, Alfred A. Knopf, New York, 1968, p. 15, 16.

GETTING CLOSER

How can people get closer and stay closer longer? One way is by working with a therapist who is fully credentialled.

However, families can work together without professional help if *each* member accepts the responsibility for his behavior and can say, "This problem is related to me: *my* fears, *my* inability to get close, *my* setting up the pain." Solution is possible when each person is looking at how *he* is contributing to the distancing. Usually we spend our time and energies blaming our mates (children, friends, business associates, etc.). I urge my patients to look for *their* responsibility in the interaction. NO BLAMING! The problem isn't what the other fellow is doing. The problem is, what defensive or symptomatic behavior am I using to keep from getting close?

Defensive behavior is something we say or think or do to keep us busy so we won't be able to look at the real problem. In a sense, we *defend against* looking at our problems; we don't know how to solve them; we avoid examining them. For example, Hugh's gambling and extra-marital episodes were a *defense against* getting close. He unconsciously used this defense instead of saying, "Ann, I'm afraid to get close to you sexually, or any other way. So I'll keep away from you by being naughty and lying. Then we'll fight so we won't be able to come closer together."

Janet's defensive behavior—being negative about herself—allowed her to be blind to what was really happening in her marriage. When she was busy knocking herself with, "There's something wrong with me—I'm selfish," she was unable to look at what was really happening. "Vic is afraid to get close, and so am I." Janet's negatives about herself kept her so occupied, she couldn't think about the dynamics of their relationship.

They were *both* involved in setting up their problems. No one was inadequate, no one was to blame, no one was "right or wrong."

Defensive behaviors do work to create distance.

If we are fighting and unhappy, lover of mine, WE have a problem, not only me. WE are frightened. WE are having difficulty coming closer. WE can solve *our* problems.

Let's work at it! Let's try to put it together—TOGETHER!

Chapter III

Two-Year-Old Eyes

We all see ourselves emotionally as two-year-olds who are struggling along in a world of enormous and capable adults. We know how easy it is to be confused—to be hurt. We feel inferior, inadequate and little; we are uncomfortable and dissatisfied with ourselves.

Using our two-year-old eyes, we see all those intelligent and sophisticated people out there. They appear to know and understand everything. They always seem to be happy and living a wonderful life. So it is normal to wonder, "What's wrong with me? Why do I have so many troubles? How is it I'm the only one who feels hopeless and helpless so much of the time? Why can't I put it all together?"

The problem is our unrealistic perception. We see our friends and neighbors smiling, telling jokes, looking well-groomed and shaved; we're certain they wake up like that. We think they spend every moment of their home and work lives smiling. Nonsense. There aren't any adults out there—no one has it all together.

WE'RE ALL TWO-YEAR-OLDS.

We start formulating our ideas about ourselves even before we are two. At that age, the man who becomes the bank president and the man who is out of work are both running around with their diapers full. Each is looking up at his wonderful Mommie. She can reach way up to the door knob. She is able to drive the magic box with wheels that takes you far away to buy ice-cream. At the age of two, no one knows how valuable and worthwhile he really is. In fact, the reverse is true. At that age, we feel stupid, confused, helpless little "poo-poo-ca-ca" people. What's even worse, while we do get older, our two-year-old eyes continue to look at ourselves in very much the same way. So, as adults, while we may be sitting in skyscrapers, ordering employees around, our very young eyes still hold a two-year-old view of ourselves.

Each of us thinks he is the only child on the playground, the only one who feels little. The rest of the adults look so efficient and effective—surely they can't be two. Never! Only me!

So we need to hide from the "big kids," the adults out there. We don't share our feelings of fright and inadequacy. We tell them we're perfect because we're certain *they are*, and we want them to like us. When we hear the people in our lives making perfect, adult-like sounds, we believe them. We believe they're smarter, more capable, sexier and better adjusted than we are. We don't question them when they give us their perfect talk and say, "I'm always happy; I'm never depressed; my children are perfect; my wife is perfect; my whole life is perfect." We don't realize this is a smoke-screen. We don't see the cover-up which is presented in the hope you won't notice how little and fragile they really feel. They too are long-legged two-year-olds, looking for your approval.

We're living in a world of hiders and liars. In my

office, both the President of the Corporation and the Chairman of the Board tell me how frightened they are. They cry with me. They lament their troubles and tell me how awful they really feel inside. If you'd met them on the street five minutes before their therapy session, they'd probably be beaming with stories about their successes.

Unfortunately, it takes a great deal of therapy to get patients to drop their smiling facades and share what really hurts and worries them. The way to fall in love with people is to share your problems with them. They'll feel relieved and then identify and share with you. However, if they're feeling too frightened and too little, they may only be able to give you their perfect talk. Try to understand their feelings and give them a hug.

Much of the loneliness in contemporary American society occurs because we are so dishonest and incapable of sharing our feelings.

We are hiders. It was a revelation living in London for three years and hearing my colleagues talk about their children. They were honest and undefensive and could share anecdotes like: "My ten-year old still wets his bed. I bet the bloody child will be wetting on his honeymoon." In Los Angeles, I have patients who would find it impossible (before therapy) to admit to anyone, including their own mothers, that their five-year olds are still not toilet-trained. Americans seem to have a ridiculous idea that being adult means we've supposed to be perfect—without mistakes, without problems.

As a therapist I say "Who's perfect, who doesn't have problems? Where are they?" To be alive, *is to have problems*. To be human and loving is to *share* them.

I've had the unusual opportunity to treat people at the extremes of the socio-economic scale. In England, Italy and Hong Kong, my patients have included the wealthy and titled classes. In my Los Angeles and London internships, I've treated people who were receiving state aid and couldn't pay anything for their therapeutic help. All people sound the same to me. When they talk honestly and share what's deep in their hearts, they sound very little, very frightened.

We're all the same. Hoping to be loved, worried about rejection, anxious about our sexual inadequacies, concerned about success in our work, wanting friends to admire and respect us, wondering and worrying if we're good parents, feeling guilty that we aren't better children to our own parents, concerned about the meaning and worth of our lives, worried about sickness and death.

We're all little and really just TWO YEARS OLD.

Let me tell you about a patient I had in London.

LORD PETER IS TWO, TOO

Peter was a member of Parliament. He had been a government leader for years. Everyone acquainted with him thought of him as a charismatic, awe-inspiring figure.

What people didn't know was how he felt about himself. How little he felt. He talked to me about his dread of the official parties he was required to attend. "I hate to go. I never am sure what to talk about. And I'm always certain people are trying to move away from me. Those damned affairs are a torture to me. I stand there, drink in hand, making charming trivia sound important and pray they won't walk away.

"Why do people continue to walk away from me in these situations? What do I do or say that is so offensive? I certainly don't know."

What he didn't understand was that he was pushing people away. Unwittingly, he signaled them to leave. When he was in these uncomfortable social settings, he would hold his hand up to his face and stare at his nails.

He didn't realize that the people he was talking to interpreted this gesture as a sign of his aloofness and boredom. Someone talking with Lord Peter and noticing him staring at his hand, would conclude that this important official was uninterested in their conversation. So they would walk away, never understanding that staring at his nails gave Lord Peter a sense of relief from his anxiety.

Peter was devastated when people left him. He always felt it was because he had done something wrong or said something awkward. He was certain that people just didn't take to him or like his personality.

When I regressed Peter under hypnosis, he was able to recall an early childhood incident when he was being chased in the garden by an older, angry cousin. Peter was frightened, tripped and fell to the ground scraping his hands. His cousin was no longer angry and helped him up with some kind words. When Peter looked at his fingers, his nails were bleeding. His cousin sympathetically put his arm around him, and they chatted warmly while walking back to the house.

It was a great relief for Peter to have the frightening experience end. He had associated (or paired) this relief with looking at his nails. He had incorporated a new magic-like equation in his memory bank:

Scared = stare at nails = safety.

Unconsciously, the incident was stored away, and he completely lost the memory as an adult. When he came out of the hypnosis, we discussed his recall. He was very eager to tell me more about it. "I hated that bloody cousin of mine. The only time he was ever nice to me was that day I fell, over fifty years ago. I've never thought of it in all this time. Does this mean that whenever I get frightened, I look at my nails as if that will help me *now*? Surely this isn't possible."

I explained that we often are conditioned with a single dramatic event from our past. For example, snake phobics often have only a single encounter with a snake and are scared of them for the rest of their lives. "You had a single encounter with a feeling of relief (and loss of fear) when you looked at your nails, and you've hung on to this association all these years. Actually, you weren't even accurate with your reality as a child. It wasn't looking at your nails that saved you. My hunch is your cousin was kind to you because you fell down and were bleeding. He probably was a little frightened himself, when he saw you fall. He might have been worried that he'd be scolded for chasing you or blamed for your accident. You, on the other hand, experienced relief when the chase stopped, and his anger ceased. You may have been thinking of this as you looked at your bleeding fingers. You put together "hands up to my face looking at my nails" means that "fear leaves and the mean cousin hugs me." No wonder you continue to look at your nails whenever you are in an awkward social situation.

"The problem is," I continued explaining, "you're using an old helpful behavior (staring at nails) in a new situation where the behavior doesn't work anymore. You thought it did that day in the garden. It's non-functional now. And what's worse is that you're scaring everybody off. They think you're a bloody snob."

No one at the state parties, looking at this stately figure with his official medals and ribbons, would have ever guessed that he was worried about being abandoned, feeling little and overwhelmed. Who would guess Lord Peter felt two-years old? He looked like he could rule the world!

After several therapy sessions, Peter was able to catch himself as his hand started up to his face while he was experiencing discomfort. One evening, when he felt frightened, instead of his finger staring gesture, he substituted these words: "I always feel like such an ass at these parties. Can't think of anything to say." The man he was talking to smiled broadly, looked around cautiously and said to Peter, "Me too, but don't tell anyone." They had a jolly conversation after that, and

Peter said he never before experienced feeling so good at a party.

Peter smiled that day as he left his sixth session saying: "Dr. Kassorla, you've convinced me that everyone at those parties feels just as frightened and small as I do. Realizing this has helped me to relax and enjoy myself so much more.

"You know, doctor, I'm almost sixty years old and I've had a full and unusual life. I'd like to share with you that one of my most valuable learning experiences has been this understanding: probably *everyone* in the world has "two-year-old eyes."

Chapter IV

Killer Talk

There are many alienating messages most of us use everyday. We are completely unaware of how offensive these messages can be. Our intentions are so good that we're surprised when people react negatively to something we say.

"I know I didn't say anything wrong. How could they misunderstand me? They must have a short fuse or they're extra sensitive."

I first came in contact with this pattern of speech, these negative communications, in Britain, when I worked with families of delinquent children. I found that the parents were using what I now refer to as "killer talk." These parents were negative and critical whenever they spoke to their children who were usually in trouble with their teachers, their peers, or the law. Without exception, I found these parents to be kind, thoughtful and loving people. But to their delinquent child, the message was often totally negative, "You're stupid, awful, can't do anything right."

Why was one child selected out of a family of three or four siblings to receive the negatives? Why was this child given the killer message and the other children given more positive, loving words? I discovered that the delinquent child, who most resembled the parents' emotional personality, was the receiver of negatives. He was their *garbage-can child*. He was the one most aware of, and sensitive to his parents. He unconsciously imitated them.

We are all so full of self-hate and self-deprecation that when we see one of our children making our same mistakes, and playing out our same personality characteristics right in front of our eyes, this is the child we unconsciously attack. It is the child who speaks to us emotionally, without words, who says, "I love you so much I'm going to be exactly like you," who receives our killer messages.

When we see our "exactly like us" child acting as we do, we try to stamp out their behavior. We attempt to destroy the part of them that is like us, the part we hate so much about ourselves. We unconsciously think, "I can't stand seeing that child making the same mistakes I do. I've got to stop him! Kill him!" This destruction is mostly verbal. Unfortunately, it sometimes includes physical punishment as well.

The *garbage-can child* in some way flashes a red flag in front of our eyes, and we start the negatives. It is likely that this happened to us when we were children. Our own mothers probably hated the parts of themselves they saw in our behavior when we were small. They gave us their negatives and killer-talk as their mothers, grandmothers and great-grandmothers did before them. This was all done without any intent to harm, but rather with love in mind and help as a goal. So for me, each generation is innocent and without blame.

The parents of the delinquent children I worked with

were good people, with flawless intentions, unaware of their destructive talk.

The problem is that we believe our mother's negative, killer messages and continue to use them in our adult lives. These messages become part of our own speech patterns which we deliver to the people we care about the most, our mates and children. With friends and associates who are far enough removed, we can be more positive in our verbal communications. With friends, we rarely see the red flag which says, "Stop that person. They are too much like ME." Friends are different enough from ourselves. Therefore, we can admire them, exaggerate all of their characteristics that we find acceptable, and over-look the personality variables that we don't prefer.

I want to list some of the kinds of negative words, phrases and messages that I find push people away. If you are able to see yourself in these examples, *good*. In therapeutic terms *seeing* is wonderful. You'll probably find some of your verbal styles among them. *Give-yourself-a-kiss* if you do. This demonstrates you're willing to change. Seeing your problems is the first step to changing; *giving-yourself-a-kiss* is the important second step. If you can identify with these examples, you may be able to realize that what you thought was just normal conversation was probably received as a killer communication.

KILLER TALK

1. *Negatives.*

Negatives are words ending in *n't*. Familiar negatives are do*n't*, ca*n't*, should*n't*, could*n't*, wo*n't*. Also in this group are *never* and *always*.

Examples: "You *never* remember my birthday . . . You *always* insult my mother . . . *Don't* listen to me, just do what you want . . . I *can't* stand your taste in friends . . . You *shouldn't* be smoking again . . . etc."

Negatives are used to tell the other person, indirectly, that you are hurt, frightened or disappointed. He won't be able to hear your message because you aren't sharing your hurt feelings but rather attacking him. Verbal attacks are so punishing, the receiver's ears tend automatically and unconsciously to close in order to protect himself from the hurt of your message. Also, the receiver can't listen to your message as he is preparing his counter-attack. The retaliation may be a return volley of killer talk, or often, it is some kind of delinquent behavior which they know irritates you.

2. *Negatives plus Questions.*

A way to compound a negative in terms of killer power, and make it even more hurting, is to put the negative in question form:

Why *didn't* you mail my letter? . . . *Don't* you ever do anything right? . . . *Shouldn't* you be losing weight? . . . Why *couldn't* you try a little harder? . . . *Can't* you ever come home on time? . . . Why is it you *never* think of me? . . . Why are you *always* making me late? . . . Why is it you *never* keep a secret?

It might be good practice for you to think a moment before you start to use the word "why," and check to see if your question is an attack.

Questions are important in verbal communications because they are a direct method for getting information. Questions don't necessarily need to be killers, but too often, they do punish and confuse the other person.

ARLENE AND DON

I have a patient, Arlene, who told me she waited anxiously all day to see her husband Don in order to share her exciting news: she had been elected PTA President. When Don came home one hour late she "hit" him with, "Why were you late? Why don't you care? Why didn't you call?" She *thought* she was saying: "I'm so glad you're finally home. I'm relieved. I've been waiting all day to share with you. I'm President."

Her questions came so fast, Don didn't get a chance to say that he tried several times to call. The line was busy all afternoon. Arlene had been phoning friends. He was so hurt by her questions, he became silent and withdrawn and didn't talk to her for the rest of the evening. Don couldn't hear Arlene's thinking. All he heard were her killer questions.

Arlene was surprised by Don's behavior when he became cold, rejecting and silent.

Arlene knew her intentions were loving, but she didn't realize that when these loving thoughts left her brain, they were blocked by her hurt feelings: "He didn't call, he doesn't care about me." Once this hurt enters the mind, unless it can be dealt with directly *out-of-your-mouth*, there is an unconscious switching of tracks or gears and the message comes out negative. This switch looks like:

Loving message intended →

hurt blocks message → (gears switch)

Negative message comes out.

The problem is that the switching occurs below the level of consciousness. Although Arlene actually delivered a negative message, she was certain a loving message came out. She was shocked at Don's chilly reaction, and concluded, "He doesn't care about my wonderful news (which, in fact, she never gave him). He thinks my life is unimportant. He thinks he's such a big shot. He thinks . . . etc." The hurt builds, and the distance becomes greater.

This is why it is so important for hurt feelings to be spoken as soon as you can get in touch with them. Hurt feelings unconsciously contaminate our messages; they come out, without our awareness, in our killer talk.

3. *Negative Prediction.*

"At the rate you're going you'll lose your job . . . If you keep eating like that you won't be able to get through the door . . . I don't see how you can possibly succeed doing it your way . . . etc."

This kind of negative communication is discouraging and tends to destroy motivation. We unconsciously reduce our effort and make the prediction in the message come true. We say to ourselves—"If you, (husband-wife-lover-parent), don't think I can make it, you're probably right. You usually are. So I'll quit."

Often the receiver of the messages is so angry, he or she unconsciously carries out the prediction as a form of retaliation, even though this is being self-destructive. The thinking is, "OK wife-husband, if you're afraid I'm going to lose my job, and if that will worry or frighten you the most, that's what I'll do. I'm so hurt you don't have faith in me, I'll hurt you back by losing my job, even though it hurts me too."

Few of us can say *out-of-our-mouths* how the negative message has injured us. This is part of the work in therapy. It is important to get hurt feelings *out-of-our-mouths* directly without destroying the listener.

Otherwise, the painful cycle continues: I kill you with my message unknowingly, you're hurt and you kill me; then I'm hurt so I kill you, then you're hurt . . . etc. Back and forth. Each partner is convinced he is innocent, his message was fine. It is the other who is insensitive and "out to injure me."

4. *Constructive Criticism.*

I believe there is NO such thing as constructive criticism in a verbal communication. Constructive criticism is *destructive.* I throw constructive criticism right out-the-window. It is a vehicle for the person who is giving the criticism to avoid looking at his own problems and create distance. By being occupied with constructively criticizing the other person, you avoid looking at what is bothering you.

Unfortunately, constructive criticism is considered by many people to be an acceptable way to relate. It is naively believed that this kind of critical communication can be helpful. Nonsense! The receiver of the criticism is often left feeling like an inadequate, stupid child. It is difficult to get in touch with your anger when you think someone is being helpful. This next case history dramatically plays out this problem.

PHIL AND RITA

I have two patients, Phil and Rita, who thrive on negative messages. Although Rita's forte is constructive criticism, they are both skilled at killing each other verbally.

Phil is an electrical engineer. Rita is an efficient and creative homemaker and mother of three, who denies her worthiness. She verbally beats herself with, "Why can't I do something with my life? I feel empty. Why am I so unhappy? Why am I so depressed?"

Rita is the big, tough, critical momma who says Phil can't do anything right. So she acts as his advisor, helper and teacher who constantly reassures him that he is a hopeless dummy who needs her constructive criticism to survive.

When Rita was ill recently, she was craving French pastry. She asked Phil if he would pick some up on his way home from work. He didn't mind leaving the freeway and went miles out of his way to a special bakery to get the pastry. When he got home, she opened the box and said, "Darling, you simply can't do it this way. The frosting is all over the box. I can't eat this mess. Let me give you a little constructive criticism: If you'll hold the box right-side up like this . . . then you won't make such an awful mess next time." Rita spoke slowly as she demonstrated the "right" way to do it. Phil was unable to tell Rita how humiliated he was by her, "Do it this way, Dummy" instructions. He was hurt that she wasn't appreciative. He had tried to please her, but she never seemed satisfied. He felt irritated and annoyed. Instead of sharing these feelings, he left the room, and a minute later he was scolding his *garbage-can-child* Charles for some minor error the child made.

Whenever Phil is angry with Charles, Rita cringes. She hates when Phil yells at their son. She explained to me in one of her sessions, "Phil's voice sounds just like my mother's when she used to scream at me. She said I always did something wrong. She was always correcting me, explaining, teaching. I hated her voice." Rita has incorporated her mother's style. Now, it is she who has the negative killer talk.

Phil can't be directly angry with Rita. That will take more therapy work. So when Rita "hacks" away at him with her negative messages he takes his anger out on their son.

When Phil came in for his next private session, we discussed the pastry caper. He was very upset. "I must be crazy. Rita means well. She's always trying to help me, yet I wanted to smash her face when she explained how to hold that goddamned box!"

"I hope so," I said, with my voice rising. "You're

not crazy. Your anger was appropriate. *Get-it-out-of-your-mouth*. Give it to her, directly!" Then I started screaming at Phil, "By the time she was finished with her 'hold-the-box-right' lesson, your testicles were cut off, and laying on the floor. Wake up! She talks to you like you're an imbecile, a four-year old retarded child."

Phil started crying, "I can't yell at her. I'm afraid she'll leave me. I love her."

"I understand, Phil," I said softly. "But you're not helping her by listening to all of her humiliating insults. If you can limit Rita by stopping the so-called constructive killer messages she delivers, it will force her to get off your back and focus on her own problems. Then I will be able to help her get to her real work—her feelings of emptiness and depression.

"Phil, your family style is too painful. Rita feels inadequate, unhappy and insecure, so you oblige her by becoming her 'garbage-can-child' and letting her dump on you. Then you're angry and feel inadequate and go out and find your 'garbage-can-child,' Charles, and you dump on him. Charles turns the painful cycle back in your laps by being delinquent in school. That's his dumping ground. When does it stop?" I wrote this diagram as I spoke.

Rita feels unhappy and inadequate, she dumps on Phil →
Phil is angry, dumps on Charles →
Charles is angry, so he's delinquent at school, which serves as his dump on Phil and Rita →
Rita feels unhappy and inadequate, she dumps on Phil →

Phil said, "I get the point. You can stop already, Doctor. I can't stand it. I see I have to give Rita my anger and stop this vicious circle. Will I ever give her that 'smash in the face' verbally, out of the mouth, as you say? Will I ever be able to stop her?"

I smiled. "Phil, you just stopped me, and I'm much tougher than Rita." We both laughed. Phil had done his work for the session. He was able to *see* the dynamics of the family pattern in action.

5. *Going South.*

A very alienating killer message, likely to result in immediate distance, is what I call "going south." Essentially, this is an *opposite* statement often made in response to someone being very open or honest. When someone says, through experience they have found "going north is best," a killer response would be "going south is the only way to go."

For example: Beverly, who is at a party, says she is having trouble with her child:

"My five-year old is impossible. He's so fresh. He said a four-letter word yesterday. I don't know how I'll survive until he grows up."

Another lady at the party named Ethel answers with a "going south" or *opposite* killer message:

"Really? My five-year-old is an angel. He's at such a perfect stage. He's so polite, so courteous—he'd never swear. It wouldn't enter his mind . . . etc."

Beverly's reaction to the other lady's going south message will probably be fury, humiliation and feelings of inadequacy. Ethel has threatened Beverly's competence as a mother. Essentially Ethel has said: "I'm a terrific mother. My child is perfect. I certainly know what I'm doing, and what the heck is wrong with you, Lady?"

Another example: Your co-worker is confiding in you:

"I can't stand this job. I'd like to spit in our boss's eye, and I'd like to throw my desk at his secretary, Miss Flat-chested."

"Going south" would be:

"Gee, I think the boss is a doll, I admire him. And his secretary—she is such a helpful, understanding dear. How can you say such . . . etc."

Another example: Your friend is telling you about the marvelous meal he had at a beautiful new French restaurant:

"I ordered escargot—you know, snails. And they were so delicious, so full of garlic and butter—what a gorgeous treat."

"Going south" would be responding with:

"Yeech! Snails! I'd rather die than eat a snail. How awful. How could you? And garlic! I'd rather die . . . etc."

There are alternatives to "going south" and they don't require that you eat snails three times a day.

For example: "I've heard that escargots are delicious from people before. I can understand how you might enjoy them."

Now, did this statement say you were going to run out and eat snails? No! Did it say you *wanted* to eat snails? No! You just acknowledged what you've heard from friends who do enjoy snails. You haven't made any commitments. You are just an understanding listener. It isn't necessary to destroy the escargot-eater in order for you to maintain your ground. You may order steak. You are *different* from your friend. That's good. His escargot is fine, so is your steak. YOU ARE BOTH FINE and you both have choice.

6. *Non-Verbal Killer Messages.*

Unfortunately, killer talk can be non-verbal as well as verbal. This opens up an entire body of physical gestures for you to look at and stop using, if you want to *stop* the distancing.

Examples: Pointing your finger at me accusingly . . . looking annoyed and aggravated with the "will she ever learn" expression on your face . . . giving me a deeply troubled, distressed sigh or moan . . . turning your head away from me or staring at your hands while I'm talking . . . raising your eyebrows while looking up towards the sky (add a moan for real killer power) . . . sitting with your back to me while you talk to someone else . . . shaking your head in a horizontal "no" fashion while I'm speaking . . . not answering me . . . walking away from me while I'm still talking . . . pulling your hand or body away from me when I reach out to touch you . . . etc.

The list of how to push people away is endless. With the start I've given you here, you'll probably be able to add, by yourself, the familiar killer messages (verbal and non-verbal) that you use daily. Good! Now get to work. If you can STOP your killer talk, you can START having more fun.

POSITIVE TALK

We understand killer messages cause pain, but what else can we say? We feel stuck! How do we change? We need new tools! I have a substitute, an alternative to killer talk. I call it *positive talk*.

When we feel good about ourselves, we don't need

to be negative or to punish others verbally or nonverbally. We see the positive things in other people. A person who feels good about himself sees beauty in others and delivers his positives, "I admire your taste . . . your house is so warm and pleasant . . . I love the feeling you've created here . . . You're a wonderful friend . . . What an excellent dinner . . . You're a marvelous cook . . . How very lovely you look . . . etc."

The better you feel about yourself, the more you like YOU, the easier it will be to feel positive about the other people in your life. You will have less need to criticize or push people away.

There is almost nothing more important in a relationship than positive reinforcement and positive talk. In the case of lovers (or dealing with your children) the best positive reinforcement is YOU.

You, person I love, are the big positive in my life! You are the most important person in my world. And if you just look at me, that is a tremendous positive; and if you smile at me or touch me, that's a tremendous positive; and if you'll say something positive about me that you sincerely believe, that's a tremendous positive and I'll be joyous!

If you see yourself being negative, it probably means you're frightened or anxious, so be easy on yourself. *Give-yourself-a-kiss* for SEEING and understanding. People thrive on their own honest positive talk. Change will occur faster when you're positive and supportive with yourself.

When you are self-critical, the negatives drive you deeper into the behavior you dislike. The more negative you are with yourself, the deeper you go, and the more difficult it becomes to change.

Give yourself positives for trying, positives for being active and positives for making mistakes. *Give-yourself-a-kiss* for having the insight to be willing to look at your mistakes. *DO-ers make errors.* Remember the year Babe Ruth led the league with sixty home runs? He also led the league in strike-outs.

If you can be kinder to YOU, it will be easier to be more understanding of the people around you. You'll enjoy more growth in yourself and your relationships.

Positive talk is a good way to come closer and put it all together with the people you need and love.

Chapter V

The Power of Honest Positives

Much of my work is based on the power of honest positives: they have motivating power, happiness power and most important, getting-closer-together power.

Honest positives are rewards. They are similar to the concept of compliments with this important addition—they must be honest. They are a kind of "positive talk" we can use when the people in our lives are engaged in behavior we like.

It is my way of explaining what in psychology is called operant conditioning or learning theory. This is a type of therapy suggesting that behavior rewarded in some way, is learned and repeated.

The theory suggests that when responses or behaviors are followed by something reinforcing—a reward—they will increase. Contrarily, responses which are followed by removal of reinforcement—or punishment—

will decrease in frequency (and delinquent behaviors often increase). Or, more simply:

Response → Rewarded → Desired Behavior Increases.
Response → Rewards Removed → Behavior Decreases.

It is important to believe the positives you give. They are *honest* positives. Don't tell your wife you like how she looks when she is wearing the dress you hate. Rather, give her a sincere compliment about something you do like. Unless the positives are honest the entire objective of getting closer together breaks down. And the communication is in serious trouble.

Many parents are already using a home-spun variety of operant conditioning. When children are naughty, parents may deliver a sharp reprimand, a quick slap on the behind or perhaps ignore the child. When children are good they receive smiles, approval, affectionate words, gestures, and maybe material rewards such as gifts or food. Praise is one of the most *powerful* of these rewards.

I was first drawn to reinforcement therapy because my mother is a very positive woman. If a ton of problems hit my mother she would say, "I'm lucky it's not two tons."

My mother triggered my interest in reinforcement theory, but it was validated by my research work, both in the United States at the University of California at Los Angeles and in Great Britain at the University of London. The research emphasis in both of these educational settings was on learning theory or rewarding desired behavior.

In 1961, I was doing field work as part of one of my undergraduate classes with emotionally disturbed children at a hospital in Los Angeles.

The children attending the clinic, which was part of the hospital, were from three to five years old and seriously emotionally disturbed.

After a few months, I noticed that the bizarre behavior of some of the disturbed children was increasing. For example, one child who came into the hospital was hitting his head. He did this rarely at first. After three months in the clinic he was a full-blown head-banger. How did this develop? When he did something incredibly sick, like banging his head against a wall or the corner of a table making himself bleed, the teacher would immediately pick him up. This reinforced the psychotic behavior and it increased. It became apparent to me that the children who were acting the "craziest" were being rewarded with the affectionate caresses of the teacher, immediately following a psychotic outburst.

If a child read quietly, he might be ignored. But if a child banged his head against a wall, the teacher would be beside him within seconds, soothing him, asking him what was wrong, telling him she understood his anger.

I thought to myself, "If I were a psychotic child in this place, I wouldn't be quietly reading a book. I'd be banging my head against the wall so I could sit on the teacher's lap. I love to be hugged and caressed."

I wrote a paper in one of my psychology classes at school suggesting that the staff at the hospital was reinforcing sick behavior which had the effect of increasing instead of reducing it. This is how my career in psychology started.

I was very lucky that the professor in my class, Dr. Ivar Lovaas, was an innovative, energetic scholar who was open to new ideas. He was interested in my observations and wanted to study them more critically in a controlled, experimental setting with a psychotic child.

We went to the Neuropsychiatric Institute on the UCLA campus and found a nine-year-old autistic child named Betty who was probably the most disturbed child at the in-patient clinic. Her parents consented to have me work with her, and she became our first research subject.(1)

(1) Lovaas, Ivar O., Freitag, Gil, Gold, Vivian and Kassorla, Irene C., *Experimental Studies in Childhood Schizophrenia: Analysis of Self-Destructive Behavior,* Journal of Experimental Child Psychology, II (1), 1965, p. 67-83.

Although I had no credentials in 1962, (I didn't receive my Doctorate Degree in Psychology until 1968) Dr. Lovaas supervised the experiment and I was permitted, under his doctoral veil, to work as the therapist. Other students were involved doing statistical work and recording their observations of my work with Betty while they watched us through a one-way mirror.(1)

I was finally able to put into practice my own ideas which were opposite in many ways to those used by the professionals at the hospital.

At first, Betty's behavior was so strange, I was frightened to be with her. I had never been alone with a psychotic patient before.

Most of the day Betty stood talking like a parrot, gritting her teeth and repeating phrases like "Betty's a good girl," "Betty's a good girl" or "Hello Betty. Hello Betty." She had no normal speech patterns. She was extremely self-destructive and had nasty welts and bruises all over her body caused from hitting herself against sharp-cornered objects. Her chin was raw where she had torn her flesh away. Whenever she was thwarted or failed to get what she wanted, she'd bang her head against the wall or jab a scissors into her skin.

My procedure was to give Betty love and tender care *only* when she acted normal. That is, I rewarded her normal behavior with my affection. The moment she did something self-destructive I turned my head away and ignored her. Within twenty-two days of two-hour daily sessions, the child had improved so much, because of my ignoring sick behavior and rewarding healthy behaviors, that she looked almost normal. The self-inflicted welts had receded and she had begun to talk more normally and to identify objects.(2)(3)

(1) Lovaas, Ivar O., Freitag, Gil, Gold, Vivian and Kassorla, Irene C., *Recording Apparatus and Procedure for Observation of Behaviors of Children in Free Play Settings*, Journal of Experimental Child Psychology, II (2), 1965, p. 108-120.
(2) Kassorla, Irene C., *From Echolalia to Spontaneity with Two Autistic Subjects.*, Master Thesis, University of California at Los Angeles, 1965.
(3) Lovaas, Ivar O., and Kassorla, Irene C., *Teaching Appropriate Language*

When I worked with Betty, there was a great emphasis on rewards. I gave perhaps fifty rewards (praise, affection, candy), to one punishment (turning my head away). Parents of delinquent children reverse this. They offer few or no rewards. They are constantly battering the child with criticism and drowning him in various kinds of verbal punishment. Verbal rewards (praise) strengthen behavior, and, I believe, increase motivation.

Betty seemed like a strange little animal when I started working with her. After only three weeks of therapy, we saw a little girl appear. She was, of course, still a seriously disturbed, psychotic child, but we were all very excited with her amazing progress.

My work with Betty in the Psychology Department of the University of California at Los Angeles lasted for two years.

Her case is one example of the tremendous power of positive reinforcement. The psychological journals are now full of similar examples using this kind of reward method with sick children.

My objective in sharing Betty's case with you is to point out the remarkable results that can be had by rewarding positive behavior. This reward theory can be applied in your daily life with your children and your mate. Most lovers spend their time complaining and nagging about what they *didn't get*. This creates distance. Rather, borrow from the research model, and reward what you do enjoy receiving, however small. Rewarded behavior grows. Rewarding a small gesture you like today, will make it a bigger gesture tomorrow.

BONNIE AND LARRY

Recently a couple came to see me. Their problem

---

and Reading Skills to an Autistic Child., Council for Exceptional Children, Portland, Oregon, April, 1965.

concerned the difficulties they were having with sex. The wife, Bonnie, frequently complained Larry was disinterested in her and didn't want her sexually. She often nagged: "How come you're not sexy like other men? . . . Why is it we so seldom make love? . . . Why can't you be more romantic?"

Finally, things started improving, and the frequency of their sex was increasing. I asked Bonnie if she was telling Larry how happy she was, how content she felt with their love making.

"No, I don't have to tell him. It's about time he woke up. I don't have to mention it. He knows."

"Bonnie, he doesn't know," I said. "He's not sure of himself sexually; few people are. Everyone feels inadequate. Don't let him play 'Blind Man's Bluff'! Tell him he pleased you.

"Remember, I told you about the research project with Betty, the autistic child? I ignored her when she hit her head and the head banging stopped. If you ignore your husband's new affectionate behavior, it too will stop. You need to reinforce him. New behavior is like a fragile little tree, which needs support. Sprinkle it generously with your positive verbal rewards and watch it grow!"

Bonnie sounded worried. "I'm not sure I even know what a positive reinforcement is. I know I'm negative and complaining, but how do I stop?"

I wrote down some honest-positives about Larry that Bonnie had told me in earlier sessions. She often talked to me about how much she loved Larry. Her positive words about him were: "I love being close to you. I love the way you feel. I adore being alone with you. You are such a turn-on for me. I love your body. I love you."

"Why are these so hard for me to say?" she asked. "I can tell *you*, Doctor, not him. Why?"

"I'm not sure 'why' Bonnie. Perhaps, like most people, your mother found it hard to accept a compliment. When someone says, 'What a beautiful dress,' you say 'This old thing, it cost only $5.95 ten years ago.'

"Even though we spend so much time buying furniture, cars, clothes, and looking attractive so we can earn praise, we all still have difficulty accepting compliments.

"Your mother may have been embarrassed when you gave her honest-positives when you were little. Or she may have been suspicious that you were trying to manipulate her to get something you wanted, even though you were sincere. So she may have punished you for saying something honestly flattering to her.

"We may never find out the reason it is so difficult for you to be positive, Bonnie. But it is clear that while you didn't learn the skill in your childhood, you *can* learn now.

"Here is your homework." I handed Bonnie the honest-positives I had written down for her about her husband.

"Practice these several times a day. You'll be able to give them to Larry directly, right *out-of-your-mouth* soon. Practice!"

Bonnie returned on the following week reporting her homework went well. "I can't believe how positive I was. I told him all the wonderful feelings I had for him. It worked! Imagine me, old negative-face being so positive. And he loved it. We had such a good week."

Using honest-positives is a way to get together and come closer to the people you care about.

Chapter VI

Recipe for Limits

Animals have a built-in sense of territory. Lions will physically pace off a prescribed area that they call their domain. If another animal or person crosses their territory, the lion will rise to defend and maintain these boundaries. It is *his* property, *his* world—you may not enter!

In a sense, people are very much the same. We too, need to specify our territories. We need to establish our boundaries or what I will refer to as "limits." In learning to communicate these limits to the others in our lives, we announce, "You can only go so far."

The first part of therapy focuses on taking care of *yourself*. New patients coming into therapy are concerned about being loved and earning approval, regardless of the cost in terms of their integrity or dignity. They are unable to get in touch with their own feelings. They focus on pleasing others. Frequently I hear patients say, "I'm so busy taking care of everyone else —I don't know who I am, what I want or what I need!" As we work together, they learn to consider, respect and take care of themselves. They take care of their own needs and wants and communicate them to the important people in their environments.

It takes time in therapy to help the patient understand that he DOES have a responsibility to himself. When he can accept the notion that it is important to consider yourself, he is more prepared to move on to the next phase. He has learned something about his own fears and inability to express feelings and will be able to take a more realistic look at others. He can begin to understand there are no more giants out there he has to please, just people like himself—frightened, fragile, two-year-olds!

The first part of therapy takes several months, because it includes the important work of limiting the people you love. One of the most difficult things to be able to say to your lover is NO. We've been trained to believe that if you really love someone, you *won't* say *no*. We grow up with this unrealistic notion, "If you care about me, you will never refuse me." We learn this from our parents who learned from their parents.

Raising a child may require sacrificing. From the moment the baby comes home from the hospital the parents' lives change, and the "sacrificing" begins.

If you're having dinner and the baby cries, you stop.

If you are making love and the baby cries, you stop.

If you are invited to the annual dinner dance and the sitter doesn't show up, you don't go.

After years of this "missing out, sacrificing" and giving up for the sake of the baby, parents feel wounded and unappreciated when they ask a child to do something for them, and the child is unwilling.

The word "no" feels like you don't care about me. In fact, most people, who may or may not be parents set up the equation:

No = No love

"How can you say no to me when I've done so much for you? I'm sure your no means you don't love me."

Because this equation is passed from one generation to the next, the child learns at an early age that if he is to be "good" and get parental approval, he must do whatever his parents ask. This feeling doesn't stop at childhood.

If you love someone and he or she asks you to do something that you don't want to do, you're afraid to say no. You are worried about his disapproval—and frightened he might leave you. So you do what he asks, even though you don't want to, hating him and yourself. You get back at him later with, "I'm the only woman in the neighborhood who does her own ironing," or "I can't stand the way your feet smell," or you'll forget his birthday, or you'll be too tired to have sex. It is sadder still when people take it out on their own bodies in the form of a psychosomatic illness. Even the common cold is more frequent with the people who can't say no.

All of these indirect methods are very self-destructive.

It is much better to say no to the person you love, and set aside for the moment this need for approval, than it is to do something you loathe and take it out in an underhanded way later. This is very damaging! When you're faced with the duty or obligation of doing something you hate, you can carry resentment and anger on your mind for years. This destroys rapport and prevents joy in the relationship.

It is essential to get your NO out. Here's a simple recipe to use without losing approval or love.

RECIPE FOR LIMITS (or NO's)

Three Positives + + +

THE LIMIT (NO)	−
Another Positive	+

For the recipe to work, the positives need to be genuine and honest.

For example: Your husband asks you to go bowling. At work he was fantasizing about how much fun it would be. He was eager to get home to ask you. He's all excited. You hate bowling. You don't even like the people who bowl. Your typical score is 37. But you want to be with your husband.

How do you say NO and let him know you still love him?

Positive 1	"I'm glad you want to be with me."
Positive 2	"It's fun being with you."
Positive 3	"It makes me feel good that you want to include me in your activities."
THE LIMIT	"Honey, I really don't enjoy bowling. I don't want to go."
Another Positive	"I love being with you and I hope we can find another activity together."

Another Example: Your wife wants to visit her mother. You don't mind doing this, but you're just not in the mood tonight.

Positive 1	"Dear, I think it's wonderful that

	you're so considerate of your mother."
Positive 2	"I like going to see her too, she's a sweetheart."
Positive 3	"It makes me feel good you want me along."
THE LIMIT	"I don't want to go tonight. I'm just not in the mood."
Another Positive	"I really like your mom. I want to plan on another night."

Another Example: Your wife "must" buy that new outfit which you can't afford.

Positive 1	"Honey, I love your taste in clothes."
Positive 2	"Everything you buy looks great on you."
Positive 3	"You're right. You really do need some new things."
THE LIMIT	"We can't afford the outfit right now."
Another Positive	"I hope that our finances are going to ease up in a few weeks so you can have something new and pretty very soon."

If your mate continues to harangue you, put your arms around him/her and repeat firmly, but even more tenderly than before, the last step of the recipe, "Another Positive."

It is so important when you say no, to realize that your partner may be very disappointed, sometimes even feel torn apart or devastated. Remember he or she is just two-years old emotionally and can't handle disappointments. So the love-positive messages need to *surround and almost caress* your NO. This way your lover (friend, child) can remember you do love him. The no is not for him but for the small event that's happening at the moment.

If you use my "Recipe for Limits," I believe you can take care of yourself by communicating your feelings—what you want and don't want—in a tender and sensitive way. This is the first part of therapy work. You will also be operating in the next phase as you will be giving attention to the feelings of the others you love. This is the important second part of therapy.

You will find this recipe works well, not only with your lover, but with everyone else—friends, children, parents and people at work. Whenever you need to say NO and still keep the love, fun and respect growing, surround your limits with honest positives.

There is a dignity in being able to say who you are, what you want and what you need. This is available to you. USE YOUR RECIPE FOR LIMITS.

Chapter VII

Insteads

Most people are aware of the concept of anger. But few of us use direct anger—we use substitutes. I call these substitutes "Insteads."

When we were small and became angry, our mothers stopped us immediately, just as their mothers stopped them. Our anger frightened them because they had no experience in dealing with these intense feelings. It was as if we were speaking a strange and forbidden language. They stopped our angry feelings during childhood, and this training continued to influence our adult lives. They assured us that only truck drivers and crazy people got angry. They insisted we lower our voices, because they were so worried the neighbors would hear. Our parents were certain we couldn't survive in our society, where the expression of direct anger is considered to be extremely unacceptable.

I think that mothers do this with the best intentions.

They feel they have to talk children out of their anger in order to prepare them for school and for adult life. They're worried that their Johnny might throw a temper-tantrum in kindergarten. They fear the teachers and neighbors will judge them incompetent.

Mother is faced with a tough job.

Anger has to be released in some way, or you would end up in a mental institution. Anger doesn't vanish when it isn't expressed. It accumulates and has a corrosive, cancerous effect on us. We start out with a small grievance. Perhaps someone has hurt our feelings. When we can't get our feelings "out of our mouths," they grow into more and more anger, expanding the way steam does when water is boiled in a teapot. Analogous to the teapot, we must have an opening or spout to release our anger-steam, or we could psychologically "burst" and become mentally ill.

Mother instinctively understands this teapot principle and knows we must have an outlet for our anger. So, mother uses what I call "insteads" for anger, and teaches them to her children. We carry these "insteads" through life, ending up with a partner whose "insteads" are similar to our own.

The healthiest way to express anger is directly *out-of-your-mouth.* If this is prohibited, there are "insteads." These are socially acceptable substitutes which our parents allow. But each substitute is costly, and in some way self-destructive.

Distancing is often the result of indirect anger. Because we are brainwashed that anger is "wrong," we learn to find our "insteads." We are so afraid of losing the people we love, instead of the rejection and disapproval, that we chose the "insteads"—instead!

The following group of "insteads" will probably be familiar to you. The list includes: over-eating, boredom, depression, criticism, physical illness, sarcasm, impotency and gossip.

OVER-EATING

Over-eating is commonly used as an "instead" for anger. (For me, alcoholism and gambling are psychologically interchangeable with over-eating.)

For example: your husband is upset because you went to play bridge instead of staying home with your child who's had chicken pox for ten days. You knew if you didn't put down your role of Florence Nightingale, and get out of the house, at least for an afternoon, you would jump out the window or explode. Your husband is furious that you left your sick child with a sitter. Because the child is feeling so much better, you think your husband is being unreasonable. You're hurt because he doesn't trust your judgment or consider your feelings.

Instead of telling him, you squelch your anger, run to the refrigerator and stuff food into your mouth. The conscious feeling may be hunger or a craving for a particular kind of food. (The unconscious feeling that results from eating is anxiety reduction.) The anger for your husband is gone when you have finished over-eating, and you probably don't even recall the incident. All that's left is anger for yourself, the fat over-eater. Being angry with your mother, father, or mate is so uncomfortable that it really feels better to be angry with YOU. It's easier to be full of self-hate than it is to be angry.

Hating and anger are forbidden. But what can we do? Nothing. We aren't allowed to express this anger, so we are left anxious and frustrated. The anxiety becomes overwhelming and makes you feel crazy. What now? You find your "instead." You over-eat and the anxiety subsides. You have found a solution! You feel momentarily comfortable again. Almost immediately, the self-hate and disgust move in. But no anxiety—no craziness. The self-hate works better. Anything works better than being full of anger and hate.

Anger = crazy = *anxiety* = great discomfort = over-eating = relief.

BOREDOM

Boredom is an "instead."

People who can't say "I'm angry" very often can say, "I'm bored." This is allowed by mother and society. It has become very chic to be bored.

When a patient comes to me and complains that he's bored, I ask him what he's angry about. Boredom is anger. If we stay with his feelings and get to the anger, the boredom disappears. Then the patient will be able to become more involved and active, which can lead to feelings of pleasure and self-worth.

Using boredom as a substitute for anger isn't very satisfying, and actually it is very self-destructive because you miss so much.

For example, you'd love to find an interesting part-time job. You're a bright, well trained and talented lady. During a phone conversation, you tell your plans to your mother. She exclaims, "What! You're going to desert your children. How could you ever think of taking a job?"

This phone call with mother ends your plans for a new job, and the possibility of excitement, fulfillment and involvement. You are really angry with your mother, but you don't share your feelings. "Instead," you stay home . . . you are miserable . . . you feel BORED!

I have no use for the word "boredom." Throw it away. LOOK FOR YOUR ANGER.

DEPRESSION

Depression is an "instead" for anger.

I have found it to be a very common substitute for anger in the United States and other parts of the world as well. People take pills for depression—tranquilizers, pain pills, uppers, and downers. Drugs are big business because depression, a prevalent phenomenon, is big business. Most of us are on intimate terms with depression, at least occasionally.

Somehow we have learned that it is dignified and acceptable to go into a depressed state, withdraw and become unmotivated—perhaps stay in bed. BUT ANGER? Certainly NOT!

Depression destroys productivity and effectiveness. If it is extreme and becomes too serious, it can lead you to a mental hospital. Remember the teapot principle mentioned earlier in this chapter. But anger? No! We've learned our childhood lesson well.

CRITICISM

Criticism is an "instead" for anger and an antidepressant. Criticism also reduces anxiety. If you are feeling depressed and can criticize someone or some thing you will feel better. Incredibly critical people are often moving away from their depressions by using criticism on others. If you let them criticize you, they will feel better. They unconsciously use criticism as it helps them to avoid looking at their own problems. But it won't work well for you. Society rewards the critical person. We dignify his behavior with words like discriminating, sophisticated, and worldly-wise. If the critical person can stop using his "instead," he'll have time to look at himself and change. Criticism creates pain and distance.

```
         anxiety
        ↗       ↘
Anger             criticism = feels better.
        ↘       ↗
        depression
```

PHYSICAL ILLNESS

Physical illness is another common "instead" for anger. The list is endless—asthma, colitis, colds, fatigue, headaches, ulcers, back problems, skin problems, flu, tumors, piles, hemorrhoids, etc. I even believe that cancer might in some way ultimately be related to the inability to express anger. Experimenters have shown that if a rat doesn't have a vehicle for anger, a chemical is produced internally which damages his body—as in the case of ulcers. However, even though I believe many physical symptoms are psychosomatically based, I always urge patients to visit their medical doctor at the first indication of a body disorder or symptom. I am willing to treat the symptom only after the medical doctor has suggested that the problem is psychosomatic.

The rate of cure has been remarkable and encouraging. For example, a patient can come to my office with a splitting headache, stomach pains, dizziness, exhaustion, listlessness, or depression. We get right to work: "Who are you angry with," I'll start the session. "I *believe* your aches and pains, but they are your 'insteads.' I want to work on your anger, not your body symptoms."

At first, they often have difficulty realizing where their anger started. Sometimes the anger is concealed; we have to hunt for it together: "Let's go down your important people list," I'll say. "Is it your children . . . your mate . . . your parents . . . your colleagues . . . etc.?" We continue to search, and eventually they are able to tune into the source of their anger. We talk about their fury, and who has hurt them. Then, as if by magic, the migraine headache or the stomach pains (or whatever) disappear. It isn't magic; it's expressing anger directly with words *out-of-your-mouth.*

Next, I encourage them to go to the person they are angry with and share the feelings, without blaming or attacking that person. "Just give them your information, don't accuse," I explain. "They probably have no idea they have wounded you. Go work it out with them." Symptoms vanish by expressing direct anger. Here are some illustrations:

Your best friend, Patricia, has had an important party and didn't invite you. You're crushed, hurt, and very angry. You can't think of anything else. For days, you have been having those terrible migraine headaches. When you're alone, driving, cleaning the house, or resting, you're fantasizing talking to Patricia. Try doing it directly. This recipe is similar to "Recipe for Limits" and includes three additional steps: (1) direct anger, (2) feelings, and (3) I want.

RECIPE FOR ANGER

Positive 1	"Patricia, you're my best friend."
Positive 2	"I love you more than any woman alive."
Anger	"I was so furious, so hurt when I heard you were having a party without me."
Feelings	"I've felt sad and depressed for days."
Positive 3	"You're special in my life."

I Want	"I want to be special for you and be included."
Another Positive	"I have the most fun when I'm with you."

I believe Patricia didn't know she was so important to you. Tell her with your positives and give her your anger.

There is a problem with using physical symptoms as an "instead" for direct anger. The person who has hurt you has no information about you. He is left completely in the dark. He may be able to see you're not well, and he may have a vague feeling of guilt or responsibility. However, he doesn't know the hurt that's troubling you.

Another example: Whenever you're out with friends, your wife has the annoying habit of answering for you when someone asks you a question. When she does this, you get those awful stomach pains and are worried your ulcer is acting up again. You want to choke her. "Instead," you keep quiet, withdraw, fume and fester. Try direct anger instead.

Positive 1	"I like the fun you and I have together when we're out with friends."
Positive 2	"Honey, I'm glad you're so interested in my conversations."
Anger	"I'm furious when you answer for me when one of our friends asks me a question."
Feelings	"It makes me feel like a mute jackass—a dummy."

Positive 3	"I know you're just spontaneous and trying to help. I like that."
I Want	"I want you to listen and let me answer the questions directed to me."
Another Positive	"I really like when you stay nearby me when we're talking, because I love your company."

My hunch is that your wife was totally unaware she was doing this. She'll probably be surprised when you tell her. She needs to hear your feelings, your anger and your positives.

Another example: Your mother likes to come to visit you and see her grandchildren. You like to have her, but you hate when she starts telling you how to clean your house, arrange your furniture, raise your children—what you "should" be doing. Your asthma always gets worse when she's there. You're afraid if you are direct with your anger, she'll be insulted and never come back. So you swallow your fury and don't say anything. You hate when you're asthmatic and have difficulty breathing. As a result, you rarely invite her over and feel very guilty about this. Try giving her your anger directly, *out-of-your-mouth*:

Positive 1	"Mom, I love the idea of you coming over."
Positive 2	"The kids are so happy when you're here."
Anger	"I haven't invited you much lately, because I get so angry

	when you tell me how to run the house or the children."
Feelings	"It makes me feel stupid and childish like I can't figure anything out myself."
I Want	"I want you to trust me to handle things in my own house without interfering."
Positive 3	"And I want you to come over more often, because it makes me happy to be near you."

Your mother thought she was helping you with her suggestions. I believe she had no idea how offensive she was being. Tell her. Make sure you surround your anger with your honest positives because most mothers are very little—just two-years-old.

Many of my patients have complained to me, "Sometimes I can't think of any positives when I'm angry. In fact, all I can think of then is murdering everyone in the whole house. I want to yell and scream. I feel crazy with your recipes and those damned positives. Is there something wrong with me?"

"Of course not," I honestly reassure them. "That's appropriate. Sometimes you do need to just blow out your anger at the top of your lungs. Fine! The total person does it all. Sometimes you'll take care of yourself and yell and scream. That's good too. You're human.

"So when you can think of the recipe and give your positives, fine. Give-yourself-a-kiss. When you want to scream and yell, that's also fine. *Give-yourself-another-kiss.*"

SARCASM

Sarcasm is fury—and another "instead" for anger. Most of us use sarcasm without being aware of the negative consequences it has on our interactions. It can be very painful to be the target of a sarcastic remark. I have patients report they can remember—even twenty years later—the smarting from the sting of a sarcastic comment they received. The pang endured.

The deliverer of the sarcasm does experience some temporary relief from his anger, even though the process is usually unconscious. My patients rarely are aware of their sarcasm and are surprised when I first call their attention to this behavior. They often say "Oh I was just kidding. I didn't mean anything by that. Can't you take a little joke?" I explained that Dr. Kassorla *can* take a joke, but the people they love will feel pushed away by their sarcastic remarks. Sarcasm creates distance.

Examples of sarcastic "insteads": Your husband is three hours late for dinner. It is the third time this week. He's in the middle of an important business merger. The minute he walks in, you give him your "instead," sarcasm:

"Look who finally came home only three hours late—the big business tycoon. Nice of you to honor us, your majesty."

Try direct anger using the above instance. Sarcasm is confusing and offers little information. The receiver has an idea that something is wrong but isn't certain what is happening. Try to keep the recipe idea in mind without strictly adhering to the steps. I want you to remember: positives, anger, feeling, I wants, and more positives. Direct anger would sound more like this:

"I'm so glad you're here, but I'm furious you're late. It's the third time this week. I could scream! I don't care about money, business, anything. I just love you. I hate when you're gone so much. I'm so lonely. I miss you so much. I want you to throw that business away and come home and love me. I hate your business. I hate it. I want you near me. That's all I care about—you."

Then try hugging him. He's tired and needs to be babied a little now. Give him a hot bath and massage his back. Be his Mommie, just for tonight.

Another example: Your wife has scraped her dessert plate clean and eaten most of your pie as well. You look at her with a feigned smile and say sarcastically:

"Guess my little vulture-face wasn't very hungry, were you darling?"

Direct anger would sound more like this:

"I didn't give you permission to eat my pie. I'm annoyed. I'm hurt you don't consider my feelings. I'm angry. I enjoy sitting next to you. That's my favorite place to be, and I like your taking an occasional bite. But I want to be asked."

Again, the goal of the communication was to offer information and included positives, anger, feelings and "I wants."

Another example: Your teenage daughter talks on the phone for hours. You and the rest of the family are sitting at the table, ready to have dinner. She is on the phone with her girlfriend. You have been holding up dinner for 15 minutes, waiting for her. When she finally comes to the table, you're angry and sarcastically say:

"Well, I'm glad the President can spare you from affairs of state long enough for you to join us. It's a good thing we aren't hungry. We're just sitting here because we have nothing better to do."

You need an interpreter to understand sarcasm. The teen-ager may think: "Was the family really hungry? Do they realize my phone calls ARE as critical as talking to the President? Were they just sitting there?"

It is less confusing when you deliver a direct message with direct anger:

"I enjoy your company at dinner time. And it really is awful to sit here starving while you talk to your friends. I'm angry with you. I want you to care about me and consider me. No phone calls during dinner. It's fun eating with you, and I want you here on time."

It is unfortunate that sarcasm is often dignified as humor in this country and considered to be clever, witty repartee. The major problem with this kind of verbal behavior is that the receiver feels assaulted, wounded and returns the attack with some kind of delinquency, lack of consideration, criticism, or sarcasm. Both of you will be so busy playing a back-and-forth sarcasm game, it will be hard to find a moment to get close.

GOSSIP

Gossip is an insidious "instead."

Gosisp does work as an "instead" for anger. However, the relief the gossiper receives is so momentary that he has to keep it going much of the time to alleviate the frustration he feels from his undelivered anger. In other words, if you gossip once, you get two minutes relief, but if you gossip ten times, you get $10 \times 2 = 20$ minutes relief from the anger. But since unexpressed anger grows and expands, the rate of gossiping has to be ever-increasing to offer relief for the "user." It becomes similar to a drug habit.

For example: Anger not expressed . . . Gossip gives temporary relief . . . Unexpressed anger grows and expands . . . More gossip is required . . . Anger, still unexpressed directly, expands more . . . Need still more gossip to maintain feelings of relief, . . . etc.

It becomes more and more apparent that gossip is a time-consuming "instead." The person listening also loses a great deal of valuable time and receives little benefit as the content of the gossip is usually a distorted partial version. The listener allows himself to be used as an outlet or a receptacle for the gossiper's anger.

The gossiper is unable to maintain important, meaningful relationships, because his reliability as a trusted friend is always suspect. Sharing precious secrets with your dear friend acts as an emotional gluing agent, bringing people closer together. This loving, sharing, open-hearted interchange is stunted when one partner feels he may be "next" on the other's list of gossiping material. Because people are reluctant to reveal themselves in his presence, the gossiper may find himself with few significant relationships.

I usually say, to the gossiper: "Let's not talk about Helen. She's not here. Let's talk about you and me."

My point is that gossiping doesn't help, because the relief is too temporary. "Insteads" don't work—direct anger does.

IMPOTENCY

Impotency is an "instead" for anger.

When couples come to me complaining that the husband either has no interest in sex or that he is unable to achieve an erection, I look for the female's involvement in the problem. I believe the male is unconsciously using his impotency as an "instead" for anger with his wife. For me it is not the impotent male, but the impotent couple.

While it is possible for fatigue, worry and various physical illnesses to be responsible for temporarily impairing sexual potency, it is *unusual* for a healthy male to become impotent before the age of 55. Kinsey reported even more encouraging data: only 27% of the male population becomes impotent by the age of seventy.(1) As a clinician, I focus on the importance of psychological factors as the critical variable in treating impotency. Research studies demonstrate that 95 to 99% of impotency is caused by psychological, rather than organic problems.(2) Behind every impotent male I find an antagonistic wife whose message suggests: "I'm fine. I can handle it, but where are YOU?"

The wife of the impotent male is generally punishing, insulting and scolding. She focuses on her husband's inadequacies which take her away from examining and changing her own life. The core of her "attack" behavior lies in her feelings of self-hate and worthlessness.

A very supportive and understanding female, who is affectionate and willing to postpone intercourse, can be helpful in bringing the problem to an end.

In a research paper discussing a surgical problem, it was noted that a man's testes had been bilaterally removed. The surgery was successful but psychological problems developed. He became impotent. He was apathetic and lost his motivation and interest in working. Some time later he fell in love with a very sympathetic and supportive woman who shared his love

(1) Kinsey, Alfred, C., Pomeroy, Wardell B. and Martin, Clyde E., *Sexual Behavior in the Human Male*, Philadelphia: Saunders, 1948.
(2) Mirowitz, J., *The Utilization of Hypnosis in Psychic Impotence.* British Journal Medical Hypnotism., 17, p. 25-32, 1966.

and was very understanding about his condition. He became potent, began enjoying his work again and was generally more positive and ambitious.(1)

Typically, the sexual education a couple with this kind of problem receives when they are children, is inadequate, negative and damaging. This compounds the problem. Part of therapy involves offering the couple new information about sex and teaching them skills which will broaden their limited point of view.

I have found that the impotent patient harbors a great deal of unresolved anger which he uses as silent ammunition to get back at his wife. Not being able to express his fury towards her openly, the wounds pile up over the years. This heavy pile up of unspoken rage acts as a symbolic anchor, weighs him down, and oppresses his sexual movements. The impotent male experiences relief from his burdensome anger when he can be instrumental in disappointing and frustrating his wife. During sex, if he is unable to perform, his wife's disappointment feels good to him momentarily. It offers him a vehicle to "sock her back" for old hurts and arguments. The problem is the cost. "Insteads" for anger are very self-destructive. The impotent male is overcome with feelings of remorse, inadequacy and self-hate.

In therapy, I encourage the husband to get his anger out through his mouth, rather than through his genitals. This takes many months of working with the couple, because expressing direct anger is so frightening for most people. What is encouraging, is that once expressed, the direct anger has a stimulating effect on sexual arousal and performance for the male.(1) The female reports increased interest, excitement and arousal as well.

(1) Rowe, A.W., and Lawrence, H.C. *"The Male and Female Gonads,"* Endocrinology 1928, 12, p. 591-662.
(1) Bach, George G., and Deutch, Ronald. *Pairing*. New York: Peter Wyden Publishing Co., 1970.

CHUCK AND HOLLY

Let me give you an example from my case studies of what happens when anger, and the anxiety that accompanies it, are not dealt with *out-of-your-mouth*:

Chuck and Holly were planning to get married in six weeks. Chuck is a TV newsman, very bright, very verbal. Holly, who is British, is a TV producer and an attractive lady. Neither Chuck nor Holly talk about feelings; they intellectualize them. So they are never quite sure what is happening. Because they are both so vocal, there is always brilliant conversation: Talk, talk, talk, but no talk about feelings. No direct anger.

Recently, Holly went away on a work assignment to London, England. In her letters, she wrote to Chuck that she went to the Old Vic Theatre twice weekly and was enjoying all the charming little restaurants. She assured him that this was what she needed, that it was a wonderful time for her seeing old friends and school chums. She said she didn't miss him and that it was very good for them to be apart. She felt she would always need occasional separations and that being apart would not hurt their relationship.

Chuck was totally unable to get in touch with his feelings of jealousy and abandonment. "My God! Thirty days away! Will she find someone else? Will she make love to someone else? Will she want me when she gets home? Will she come back or decide to live there?" He didn't consciously experience any of this jealousy, anger or fear. All he wrote back to Holly was that he was fine, and he didn't miss her either.

When Holly went away, it frightened Chuck. He didn't share this with her.

She didn't reassure him enough, didn't call him and seldom wrote. She played it cool; she was busy; she didn't need him. And here Chuck was thinking, "Where is this woman I love? How can she go away and leave me for thirty days? She doesn't care about me. Screw her! I don't care about her either. I don't want to get married next month—maybe never!"

When Holly came back, Chuck called off the wedding. Invitations had gone out weeks before, and all the plans were set. Holly was shocked and very distressed. He said, "You know, we don't have to get married so soon. What's the hurry? There's plenty of time." Holly was devastated by his reaction, but she didn't say a word. Coolly, she kept talking about her great work-holiday.

When I asked Chuck if he was hurting, frightened or jealous, he profusely denied it. Angry? "Of course not," he insisted. "She was too busy to phone or write. After all," he assured me, "Holly and I are mature adults—not given to emotional outbursts like anger. We're too civilized."

Nonsense, he wasn't upset! Not much! When Holly came back, he completely obliterated her, wiped her out emotionally with his, "Baby, the wedding is off." How's that for an "instead" for anger?

Interestingly enough, this is the second time around for Holly with an intellectual, non-angry man. Her first husband Clive, often commented that anger was vulgar. Clive's "instead" for anger was finding a mistress. Every year he had a new one, and frequently Holly would "accidentally" find out. There would be lipstick on his collar or mysterious phone calls late at night. When he'd say he was working overtime at the station, a Barclay card would verify he was at a romantic little restaurant just outside of London. The Harrod's Department store bills showed charges in the women's sportswear section that Holly didn't make, etc.

After fourteen years of "accidentally" finding out there were other women, Holly ended the marriage.

The point I'm making is that Holly was involved with two men who couldn't express their anger to her directly, *out-of-their-mouths*. Both of them used "insteads" that were very agonizing for Holly to experience.

Direct anger may sting for a moment, but "insteads" can cause a lifetime of pain. Direct anger is the least costly route to travel. My patients report they are able, after considerable work, to be furious with one another at 10:00 a.m. and be laughing and having fun by 10:05. They feel finished and are ready to be loving when they can express their anger. I hope you will be able to get anger directly *out-of-your-mouth.*

Say to your partner, "We have so much love in the bank, so many beautiful moments—we can afford the anger. Besides, the "insteads" are deadly to ourselves and to our relationship."

"Insteads" create distance and prevent us from coming closer to the people we love.

Chapter VIII

Flying Blind

By "Flying Blind," I'm suggesting that most of us spend much of our communication time mind reading. We don't verify the meaning of what is being said. Rather, we make assumptions about what we *think* we are hearing. We seldom check. We're often confused, and we Fly Blind.

The drama of Flying Blind was represented clearly when Steff and Linda came to see me. "Dr. Kassorla," Linda said enthusiastically, "When I heard you say, on your television show, that you sometimes wanted to throw your daughters out the window, I had to laugh. I said to myself 'Linda, that woman's for you. She'll really understand your problems.' I want to throw my six kids out of the window—all the time."

Linda, looking disgruntled, turned to her husband and complained, "Why was I dumb enough to have six kids just to please you? I'll never know! It's all your fault. I'm so miserable, over-worked and exhausted."

Steff looked astonished, "What do you mean, my fault? You mean you didn't want six kids? I thought you loved having so many kids. I thought that was all you lived for. NOW she tells me. I wanted to have *two* kids, not six!"

Linda looked like she had been struck down. "Me? I hated having so damned many kids. I thought it was all your idea. Why do you think I'm always bellyaching about them?" She started crying, "I've always felt overwhelmed and trapped. I thought I was pleasing you. I thought you wanted your own little army. Not me, I've always wanted to go back to work and to travel and . . . etc."

After they had gone back and forth for several minutes, I interrupted. "This isn't anybody's fault. You two have each been guessing what the other wanted and needed. This never works unless you have a crystal ball and can perform magic. You are both assuming you know what the other one is thinking. Check! ASK your partner what he wants. You are *both* Flying Blind!"

Linda stopped crying. "I was afraid to say anything. I never dreamed of checking. I was positive I knew what you wanted. I was afraid to tell you I didn't want so many kids . . . frightened you'd want to leave me and find a real homemaker . . . a real woman! Actually, I hate almost everything about the house—cleaning, cooking, taking care of the kids. I never told you this before, but I hate all of it."

Steff laughed, "I don't blame you—I'd hate it too. In fact, I love getting away from the kids every morning when I go to work. I can understand why you'd rather go to work. I know it's really rough for you."

This was the first time Linda was able to share real feelings. Most people are afraid to talk to each other. They fear that if they are honest and tell the person they love what they're thinking, that person will go away. Steff didn't go away. Actually, he was very understanding. Sharing feelings brings people closer.

It's tragic how few lovers can communicate. Even people who have been together for a long time are frightened. Like Linda, they think, "How can I really tell the person I love my deep-hidden secrets? If I tell him how I really feel—the truth about myself, he'll think I'm abnormal, selfish and irresponsible. What's worse, he'll think I don't love him and he'll leave me." Even people who have been married as long as twenty years are still frightened to share their true feelings.

The second session with Linda and Steff opened with some positive messages. They were both feeling better. It took only a few minutes, however, before they were at it again, complaining and screaming about how neglected and unfulfilled they felt. Each blamed the other for his problems.

"No one is to blame," I interrupted. "You're both so dead. Try to talk about your feelings. Neither of you knows what the other wants. How about some information? You're so busy complaining, attacking and defending, there's no time for sharing. Each one of you thinks he's the only neglected flower."

Linda attacked, "That reminds me. You want to hear feelings, Doctor? OK. Steff, I felt awful when you forgot my birthday last month. You couldn't even bring me a single rose; you're so damned thoughtless."

"A rose!" Steff defended. "That's the last thing I'd do when I know you're so allergic to them. I'd never bring you roses! Do you think I want to get killed!"

Linda looked suspicious, "What do you mean, allergic? Where did you get that idea? I'm not allergic. I love roses."

Steff continued his defense, "What do you mean, how do I know? You told me! When we were on our honeymoon, you broke out in a rash and said you were allergic to flowers."

"Christ, that was eighteen years ago! I can't believe you still remember that! I didn't know what the rash was, and I was afraid you'd think I had a contagious disease or something. I adore flowers. Don't you know that? I just made up that rash story."

Steff was standing up now. "How am I supposed to know, damn it? I'm no psychic. It seems like a thousand years since you said anything to me about flowers. I just assumed you hated them. And speaking of feelings, I was always worried on our honeymoon that I didn't turn you on sexually. You didn't want to get near me for over a week. You seemed so disinterested."

"You *do* turn me on Steff. You always have. I 'guessed' we didn't have sex the first few days because you were too shy to make a move," Linda replied. "So I just acted like I wasn't interested and that sex wasn't important to me. I didn't want you to look bad. I was afraid you'd feel embarrassed."

"Look bad!!" Steff shouted, "I wanted sex. I wasn't shy. I was ready and eager all the time. I 'guessed' you needed more time. I thought you were shy, so I didn't push."

"Me!" Linda said angrily, "I'm as shy as a bulldozer. I was afraid to push *you*! I didn't need time. I was afraid you couldn't perform!"

"This is like Laurel and Hardy," I interrupted again. "Neither one of you has a mouth except to complain and accuse. This guessing-game has been going on for eighteen years. You two 'Innocents' are nauseating. I've had it. You're both great at blaming and feeling annoyed. I want you to try something else. I want to give both of you an alternate way to go. Study this. Here's your homework." This is what I wrote down for them.

HOMEWORK

1) Share information.
2) Stop guessing, blaming, attacking.
3) CHECK on what you THINK the other one is saying. Check it out to make sure.

4) Instead of attack, ask yourself, "Have *I* set this up by not making myself clear, by not giving enough information? Am *I* responsible for my partner not understanding?"

"When I said earlier, 'talk about feelings,' Linda, you started attacking Steff about your birthday and your 'no roses.' I want you to try another way that includes YOU taking the responsibility—and I'm talking to each one of you when I say YOU. In your case Linda, if you can try to understand and say to yourself, 'What set of circumstances am I creating to inhibit him from buying me roses? *How have I set it up?*' With this in mind, you then could say to Steff, 'How have I set this up? Have I discouraged you?' You see, for me, there's no blame. Rather, try to get some information and *take the responsibility* for the messed-up communication. Each of you take the responsibility.

"Then, Steff, you could help by giving Linda any information you remember about the incident. No blame. It's your problem, too, Steff. Each of you is responsible if the communication breaks down. It would be your turn to see if you misunderstood. Maybe you should have checked again to see if she's still allergic. There hasn't been a single incident of rashes in eighteen years. Also, flowers aren't the only present you can buy. You knew forgetting her birthday would cause a conflict. You may have unconsciously wanted to start a fight. Perhaps you were frightened of getting close.

"The point is, each one of you needs to say, 'How am I responsible for this?' Each partner needs to concentrate on how he might have communicated more clearly. Place the emphasis on 'How was I confusing or ambiguous? How did I foul up the interaction? How did I muddle things up? Your partner is fine. Stop blaming—start communicating. As long as you attack and defend and accuse, no progress can be made, and neither of you can change."

As a therapist, I'm very concerned about guessing, because most of the time people guess wrong. Guessing causes many of the fights that patients bring in to discuss with me.

This next example is typical of many of the problems I hear daily from patients. It may help you understand more about the complex energies involved in guessing.

You and your wife are sitting and quietly reading. You've had a pleasant dinner. She's feeling very good. Suddenly, she jumps up and leaves the room. You hear the dog barking and you're certain she jumped up to feed him. You think, "She's forgotten again. I asked her to feed the dog in the morning. Here it is 8 p.m. and she's just feeding him now. She ignores me . . . doesn't hear a word I say."

When your wife comes back, you say something sarcastic to her, something unrelated to your hurt feelings. This is your indirect way of expressing anger. She retaliates and says she's bored, which is her indirect style of hitting back. Neither of you is able to share feelings. She thinks you're angry at her because she isn't wearing shoes. She remembers you told her to wear shoes, so her nose wouldn't run. She hates when you sound like her father. That's why she left the room—to get a Kleenex for her running nose. She didn't want you to scold her. And this is the way evenings go—full of misunderstandings and unnecessary pain. Each partner is guessing what's going on. Guessing is not reality.

Check. Don't guess. Check to see if there is something worrying your partner. Check to see if he (or she) is angry. Check to see if you've done something to upset him. He is right there. ASK him. Don't Fly Blind.

This inability to communicate often occurs in sex. Each person has the notion that his partner has ESP and will automatically know what he wants emotionally and sexually. This just isn't so!

The following vignette illustrates how insufficient communication (or Flying Blind) in sex can create distance and disappointment.

I dated Fred before we were married and Fred loved his stomach rubbed and juicy kisses on his fingers. I figure all men are alike so I'm sloppily kissing your fingers and briskly rubbing your stomach. Well, you're not Fred and you hate it. But you've never told me. You are waiting for me to read your mind and please you. In ten years of marriage you've never said you were dissatisfied. So here you are disappointed and frustrated. Instead of getting what you want—you're waiting and suffering with your wet fingers and irritated stomach.

When they first begin therapy, many patients hide their feelings. They're certain they are clearly delivering their concealed or unspoken messages. When they do speak, they are unaware of how their communication is coming across. They don't realize that they are often saying something inappropriate or insensitive. Much of the work in therapy deals with helping patients develop more workable methods of communicating. In doing this, the patient learns to offer others more information about his feelings and thinking and in return, gets more information back from them. This allows him a better understanding of what's happening in his relationships.

We need to share ourselves with the people we love—our thoughts and our feelings. It is important to let your partner know you. Check with each other. Don't guess. Don't "Fly Blind."

Chapter IX

Marrying Your Mother

We were only five minutes into the therapy session, when my patient got up from his chair and started pacing back and forth. He was irate! He looked annoyed and angry. I had just suggested to him that he had married his mother—that we all "marry our mothers."

Even after explaining that I meant "psychologically similar mother," the patient still found it a difficult and incredulous concept to consider.

"Are you kidding? My wife is nothing like my mother. That's ridiculous! Married my mother! This time you're way off, Doctor."

After many weeks of work, patients begin to understand that the ways they are dealing with their mates are similar to their old patterns of interaction with mother. They come to accept the concept that we do marry our "psychologically similar mother." This is normal and we all do it.

Here again, I use the word *mother* in the symbolic sense. In these terms "mother" is a composite of mother and father in relation to all the ideas, values, rituals, social behaviors and emotional patterns we learn from them as we are growing up.

Regardless of our sex, each of us marries our "psychologically similar mother." I say "psychological" because the person we marry usually in no way looks like mother, and may not behave like mother. But, in fact, the person we marry is mother's psychological twin. In emotional terms, they are similar to mother in the way they handle distance, loving, affection, comforting, support, pain, suffering, fear of rejection, anxiety, guilt, death, anger, etc.

This is how we come to marry mother. In our family, as we grow up emotionally, we learn what psychological routes and maps we are permitted to use. Each family shapes and allows its child to *travel* into certain areas of feeling and experience. They emphatically prohibit *travel* into other emotional places.

Essentially, parents present a large map to the child during infancy, and state symbolically (there is no real speech since this is all unconscious behavior,) "There are *our* roads—our emotional and feeling *roads* of *travel*. Mother decides on the route, and we follow. "You may use them exclusively for your *travel*. These are the GOOD, RIGHT, PROPER, SANE, DECENT roads which Daddy and Mommy take. We'll love you, praise you, and value you if you travel along these appropriate routes with us. Do not consider any other roads. On them you will find harm. If you do consider them, we will desert you. You will go crazy; you will die psychologically and you will be lost forever. Listen! Beware!"

When I say that a man finds someone like his mother to marry, I include men and women, both heterosexual and homosexual. We all look for, find and "marry our mothers" regardless of our sex or sexual practices. We choose a partner whose emotional makeup is close to mother—her psychological match.

No matter how many times you marry, you find your psychological mother. If you obtain six divorces, you have found six mothers; because it is mother with whom you first learned to relate. She was the one who was there, leaning over the crib, to receive your first smiles and gurgles.

We all learn how to interact with another person from our experiences with mother, in our earliest days in the crib.

There is an enormous range of reinforcing, ignoring and punishing behaviors that mother can engage in with the new baby. There are great extremes the mother can employ in raising the child, which range from one end of the behavioral continuum to the other. Along this continuum, each one of us finds his place as a parent and proceeds to shape his child in the fashion he decides is good and workable for him. Therefore every child learns to *travel* in step to the pace laid down by mother.

I want to demonstrate that the range of extremes, in terms of rewarding or punishing the child, is very wide, (not that any of the following examples are *good* or *bad*).

During the first verbal communication with the infant's bubbles and goo-goo's, the shaping process starts. With some infants, every sound they make is picked up, reinforced, laughed at and imitated by mother. This child will probably be a "talker"—maybe too much. With others, their early verbal communications are ignored or the child is told to be still, go to sleep, settle down or a pacifier may be inserted into his mouth to keep the child quiet. This one may develop into the "silent" type. One child's cry immediately signals the mother to run to his aid; another mother lets the child cry it out. One mother is in attendance, pushing the child on his swing and fulfilling his every command;

another mother is pushing the child outside to play alone.

It is mother who shapes the child. She is the one who structures the emotional and physical conditions under which the child is raised. She provides all the rewards, food, comfort, body contact and stimulation.

The child learns to walk at the mother's pace. Mother is the big one, the boss, the holder of all the controls. The child is shaped *her* way; it is the way she can tolerate, be comfortable with and live with.

Imagine that your mother was, of all things, a mechanical, steel, circular gear with spoke-like teeth all around the edge. Imagine also, that these teeth were all of different shapes and sizes, each representing one aspect of your mother's psychological personality such as the amount of distance she needs, the amount of love, fear, guilt, pain, affection, anger, etc.

Now imagine that you, as a baby, were a blank circle of very soft clay. From the time you were born, you and your mother, toothed and untoothed gears of hard steel and soft, pliable clay. You rotated against each other. Within a very few years, her strong steel teeth ground their counterpart right into your much softer material, and you began to mesh smoothly together. As this psychological process continued, your soft clay hardened and became firmly set.

Later, after your clay is fixed and solidly formed, you go out to find your mate. You will probably reject anyone whose psychological gears do not fit exactly right with yours. You will be attracted to someone whose gears are compatible with yours.

It is with a partner whose meshing is closely fitted to mother's that you will be satisfied and comfortable and be able to use the emotional skills you have.

DAN THE DO-er

I have a patient, Dan, who is a financial consultant. He's extremely verbal and has a great facility with words. He is a competitive, successful, award-winning high-achiever.

He told me of an incident that occurred recently. His story helps us to understand how his talking and high-achievement behaviors developed. They were reinforced during his childhood and shaped by his mother.

He was taking his mother, whom he saw on rare occasions, to the theatre one night. He always thought of his mother as a "strong, controlling, talkative and truck-like woman." As they were going up the escalator steps, no one was talking. Dan's mother turned to him, smiled, and said, "Tell me, Darling, what happened to you today?" He started to answer, then said to himself, "I don't feel like talking now." He hugged his mother and replied, "We'll talk later."

He continued to notice that at every quiet moment during the evening, his mother would interrupt the silence with, "Tell me something nice you're doing," or "What dragons did you conquer today?" or "Tell me something interesting you know."

He said that he understood by the end of the evening why he was always running, talking, active. "I guess I thought I had to collect important dialogue, achievements and awards to give my mother during those moments of silence.

"I didn't realize until tonight that she probably feels uncomfortable and anxious when no one is talking, and she reduces this anxiety by getting me to perform and make conversation. I feel like a jack-ass. Have I been killing myself all my life, studying too hard, working too hard, just so I'd have some material to present to my mother to break the silences SHE couldn't stand?"

Dan had reached an important place in his therapy. He was starting to *see* or gain insight into what was happening in his relationship with his mother.

It is critical to remember that Dan's mother was also shaped as a child by her own mother. Dan's grandmother probably felt uncomfortable whenever she saw Dan's mother resting and sent her off on some chores. The chain is endless. We could each go back to earlier ancestors and see how they influenced their children's behavior. Dan's mother is not to blame. She's using the methods that came from her own childhood package.

In our private sessions, Dan related vignettes from his early experiences which helped to clarify how his behavior was shaped by mother:

"Whenever I'd lay down on my bed for a minute to rest, she'd be on my neck with 'Do your homework . . . take out the trash . . . feed the dog . . . don't put off until tomorrow what you can do today . . . busy hands are healthy hands' . . . etc."

"If I'd bring home an "A", paper, she'd say, 'That's fine, I wonder what you're going to do next; you're so wonderful.' I'd feel that I immediately had to get to work and do something else to please her. I couldn't go out to play; I couldn't rest; I was always studying."

During a session one afternoon, Dan came up with this insight, "I can't believe it! My wife sounds just like my mother! 'What are you going to do next, darling? I know you'll think of something wonderful . . . Honey, I can't reach this, will you get it for me? . . . Dan Darling, you do the checks; you're so good at it.' Nothing has changed, I still can't rest. I kill myself at work, and when I come home, she has one thousand jobs ready for 'Darling Dan.' "

It is important to understand and be able to look at the concept of "marrying your mother" when considering the entire picture of distancing, getting closer and change.

Until Dan was able to understand the dynamics of the relationship he had with his mother, no change was possible for him. He was fixed in the role of the workhorse—over-burdened, and over-achieving.

Step one of change was available to him when he was able to see that his behaviors were shaped by his mother. *She* couldn't stand the silences, so *he* had to talk. *She* was uncomfortable with his resting, so *he* had to be busy with chores or studies.

I've organized the formula Dan used for changing into the following steps. Dan put it together this way, and so can you. Try to remember the main parts: seeing, no blame for them, no blame for you, *give-yourself-a-kiss*. And I mean, I'd like you to actually give yourself a kiss!

CHANGE

A. Step One: SEEING

The patient gets an understanding of the dynamics of the interaction when he starts to see the "mother-child-gears" in motion. The movement is like a chain or sequence of events. The patient needs to see this chain before he can stop his old behaviors.

Mother's anxious, due to silent moment → she cues child to talk: "Tell me something interesting." → child talks → mother feels less anxious.

B. Step Two: NO BLAME FOR THEM

For change to occur, it is important that the other person in the interaction—in this case mother—is left without blame. Her intentions were pure and good. She was unaware and unconscious of her early history and the dynamics of her interactions with *her* mother. She did what she could to become less anxious and more comfortable: she unconsciously cued the child to talk and then rewarded him for talking.

C. Step Three: NO BLAME FOR YOU

For change to occur, it is important that Dan be *without blame* in his own eyes. He was innocent as a child. His mother was his big *positive*; she had all the comforts and rewards he wanted. He did need her approval. He had no place else to go for love, so he had to perform for her and stop the silence.

It is at this point I urge my patients to literally *give themselves a kiss* for having the insight to see the above scheme. No self-blame—but rather, self-support and self-affection in the form of a kiss. Try one after each of the above steps. It feels good. Just kiss your fingers and then pat your cheek with your kiss. That's how you *give-yourself-a-kiss*!

Once Dan was able to put together the above, he could go to the next phase and bring his childhood interactions with his mother into his contemporary life. You'll remember that he was able to stop the old behavior patterns on the escalator. He didn't fill the silence when his mother felt anxious and cued him. Rather, Dan gave her a hug, which was a useful alternative, since affection and hugging can serve as good anxiety reducers.

For the first time in his life, Dan didn't have to perform to keep his mother comfortable. His behavior now looks like this:

Mother's anxious, due to silent moment → she cues

child to talk → child doesn't feel like talking → instead, he gives mother affection and hugs → mother feels less anxious.

Both Dan's and his mother's needs were satisfied—he wanted to be silent, and she wanted to feel less anxious. However, in this example, he was able to realize he had an alternative route. He didn't have to do it mother's way. He was able to make an adult decision and do it his way. He took care of his own wants and needs and still considered his mother.

Now when Dan lies down to take a rest, and his wife urges him to do one of her "thousand jobs," he says to himself, "She's probably worried or anxious about something else that doesn't have anything to do with me. By nagging me about the jobs, she can stop thinking about her own problems for awhile. I'm glad to help her feel less anxious, but not by killing myself. I'll find an alternative way."

Dan will ask his wife to join him when he's resting. He hugs her quietly. This helps to reduce her anxiety. He does help and consider her. And Dan gets what he wants and needs—some rest.

By understanding the concept that WE ALL MARRY OUR MOTHERS, Dan was able to *see* how his interactions with mother were influencing his present behavior with his wife. He doesn't need to be talking, performing and achieving all the time. He can relax more now. His insight has allowed him to stop the old "meshing" and introduce new patterns. This has enabled him to have a more rewarding relationship with his wife.

Chapter X

Extra-Marital Affairs

The extra-marital affair is a way of life for many Americans. It is even more widespread for people in other parts of the world, which may be due to the legal, social or religious restrictions on divorce that exist in other countries.

Most of us are taught from childhood that sex is "dirty." Traditionally, the role of the good mother has been to keep her daughter from becoming pregnant and her son from participating in fathering a child out of wedlock.

Mothers are faced with the overwhelming task of preparing their child for school, for friendships, for loving, for marriage—for his entire adult life—*and*—for sexual activity. Her task is almost impossible from the start. According to the rules of society, as she understands them, she's not to offer any accurate sexual information during childhood or adolescence. She is also required to make certain that no sexual behavior will occur. Then, according to her traditional formula, it is necessary for mother to send this sexually uneducated and ill-prepared child off to marriage as soon after puberty as possible.

Unconsciously, every mother understands the irresistible appeal of sex. She knows the tremendous job it is to keep the child away from the beauty and pleasure of sex.

It's a no/yes kind of dilemma: no sex or sex education during the growing years. Then, marriage and the uninformed, awkward and inexperienced young adult is suddenly expected to be comfortable with this strange and forbidden activity. For years sex was a "no-no" and INSTANTLY it's supposed to become a "yes-yes." How do you institute this no/yes kind of thinking and get an easy, normal transition into adult life? *You don't.* There is no way a parent can prepare a child for such a complete reversal of attitudes toward sex. The marital "I do's" do not change "sex is dirty" to "sex is healthy." The well meaning parent inadvertently prepares his child for unsatisfactory sex by offering early sexual information full of negative untruths, inaccuracies and forbidden associations.

How does a mother fall into this problem? The pattern develops something like this: she doesn't have much time to shape and mold the child in the way she feels is "right." She's worried that she doesn't have the wisdom or strength. And the job seems inconceivable when she first views the infant and says to herself, "This baby is an instant gratifier. He doesn't postpone anything. He defecates, urinates, cries—*the minute he gets the urge*! How will I get him to stop being sexual, the *minute he gets the urge*? How do you teach him to postpone gratification?"

Mother finds the solution by using a process called "mediated generalization." This essentially means that if you have one idea established in the child's thinking, you can attach and associate a new *unestablished* idea very quickly by merely pairing the new concept with the old. For example, the mother has established the concept that *dirty* is bad: we don't eat with *dirty* hands; we don't put that *dirty* food from the floor in our mouths; we don't touch *dirty* things; mother cleans the *dirty* house, etc. Dirty is usually firmly established as "bad" by the time the child is two years old.

As the two-year-old moves out into his expanding world and begins to interact with other children, mother is able to attach the new idea of sex to the old concept of *dirty*. Once mother makes the connection we have a new association (via the mediated generalization). Sex takes on all the established attributes of dirty.

Sex = dirty = bad = not for nice clean children.

For example, the child may be fondling his genitals as he watches T.V., and the mother will say sharply, "Stop that, it's dirty," or the child may comment about an incident in a toilet at the playground concerning the size, shape, etc. of another child's genitals. The mother abruptly intercedes with, "Don't talk like that—it's dirty." Or perhaps when the child is bathing with a sibling they may try to touch and examine each other's genitals. The mother slaps their hands with, "Don't ever do that—it's dirty."

The child learns that anything to do with genitals—his own, his pet's, anybody's, is naughty, and that sex is connected with dirty words. Mother feels overwhelmed with the "stop-sex" job ahead. She understands the conflict because she knows that touching your own body feels good, and that sex-play at any age is fun. So she over-teaches and over-reacts.

Medical doctors assure us that masturbation is a normal activity.[1] Yet, when a mother walks in on her child masturbating, which is a healthy behavior, she

(1) Harsh, C.M. and Schrickel, H.G., *Personality, Development and Assessment*. The Ronald Press Col., New York, 1950, p. 57, 126, 330.

typically reacts with disgust and horror. The child gets the idea that touching himself or herself is bad. Evil. Dirty.

From then on, it is a series of more over-reactions on the part of the well-meaning mother. For example, a mother and child, walking leisurely down the street, see two dogs copulating. Suddenly the mother grabs the child's hand, turns his face away from the direction of the dogs, and starts walking away, very rapidly. Why? It is a healthy, normal behavior for dogs to copulate in the streets. It is completely acceptable in the circles of the Blue Ribbon 400 of the dog world.

The reason I use this example is that it is surprising how many patients have recounted similar incidents to me—how mother forcefully turned their heads away from the so called horror of dogs, or other animals copulating. Forcing a child to turn his head away might be appropriate if someone were dismembered in an accident. Turning the child away from the "disaster" of animals copulating seems ridiculous.

The list of negative associations and words linked by mother with sex grows as the child gets older. "How horrible! How nauseating! How disgusting those animals are! They don't understand. Right out there without shame. That's why *they* are dogs and we are people." Sex is stamped as "inappropriate-sinful" behavior. "Not for nice people like us."

Most of our sex education during childhood is picked up in unrelated scraps and pieces from our equally uninformed playmates. We gather these distorted bits of information, along with whatever we can learn from our parents, thereby developing our sexual frames of reference. We know the four letter words often before we can even define them. For example, most children are familiar with the word "whore" before they understand anything about sex. They're really not sure what they're saying, yet they make the association and have the genuine feeling that whores are particularly bad, and good people are non-sexual.

Whore = dirty = lower class = animalistic = distasteful = wrong.

Good girl/boy = clean = decent = non-sensual = non-sexual.

We are taught as children the myth that "only whores and dogs do it." We bring this myth into our clean marriage with our nice husband or pure wife. And we look for and marry the *clean* partner who is not sensual. How can we have "dirty" sex with a "clean" partner?

This hypocrisy is so drummed into us, that it is not uncommon for a prostitute to behave "morally" in her own love relationship. She will refuse to perform certain acts, such as oral-genital sex with her own husband, although she engages daily in this activity in her work.(1) Even the professional prostitute holds the belief that sex has to be dull, non-sensual and "clean" in marriage.

For mother, it is an uphill battle. She's fighting all the way to limit the child sexually, according to what she believes is appropriate. As the child gets older, but is still too young for marriage, her problems increase. The media never ceases bombarding her children with advertisements for silky skin and exposed cleavage. In fact, research suggests that since 1950, there has been a steady rise in the percentage of sexual references in popular periodicals.(2) It is mother against the media in many cases. She tries to cool the fires of x-rated movies and unsolicited pornographic magazines. She moans, "How am I ever going to keep my child non-sexual and under control with all the outside focus on sex and stimulation?"

As the child gets older, it becomes even worse for mother. The child moves farther away from her and is

(1) Kinsey, Alfred C., Pomeroy, Wardell B., and Martin, Clyde E., *Sexual Behavior in the Human Male,* Philadelphia: Saunders, 1948.
(2) Scott, Joseph E., and Frankel, Jack L., *Sex References in the Mass Media,* The Journal of Sex Research, 9, No. 3, 1973. p. 196-209.

strongly influenced by peer groups and sexual data—books, magazines, movies and the real thing. The sexual education they get with peers is extremely inaccurate and incomplete. This can work against healthy behavior. In fact, research suggests that promiscuous girls (i.e. sex at thirteen or earlier, etc.) have little information regarding sexual matters or general physiology.([1]) What's even sadder is that few children today, dozens of years since this research was gathered, get substantial, correct and adequate sex educations from their parents.

It doesn't take many trials for the sex = dirty equation to be firmly established in the child's framework of reference.

Finally, the child becomes the adult, marries and the time for transition is presented to him. Sex now becomes a "yes" activity. Unfortunately, the equation "sex is a dirty no-no," has been firmly based in early thinking and is not so easily erasable. The young adult has been trained *not* to enjoy normal, healthy sex in marriage and has been prepared for the distancing, guilt and self-hate of EXTRA-MARITAL AFFAIRS.

LOUISE

I'd like to share a case history about a patient named Louise which illustrates how this early childhood implant: sex = dirty, affects adult sexual behavior. Louise is married. She's in her early thirties.

When she was six, her mother discovered Louise and her male cousin (also six) playing "doctor." Their pants were off and they had very briefly examined each other's genitals. Then they decided to play "bakery" and were collecting their little spatulas, knives and other cooking tools when mother walked in HORRI-

(1) Lion, Ernest G., Jambor, Helen M., Gorrigan, Hazel G. and Bradway, Katherine P., *An Experiment in the Psychiatric Treatment of Promiscuous Girls,* San Francisco: Department of Public Health, 1945.

FIED. "Why are you holding those knives? What's happening? Why are your pants off?" Mother sounded like she was viewing Dracula at a sex orgy, with knives ready for the castration sequence. It was only a perfectly normal short-term interval of: "Let me see yours and I'll let you see mine." The sex play or curiosity with her cousin lasted about two seconds but the *horrified* look on mother's face was remembered vividly by Louise for twenty-five years.

She was afraid to play doctor again because the "horror-association" related to sex was implanted by mother. Her next unfortunate sexual experience occurred as a young teen-ager, when mother accidentally came upon her when she was masturbating in her room, with the door closed. Mother entered unexpectedly and it was like recycling the six-year old event. Mother was horrified, "That's not healthy. Go wash your dirty hands. That's perverted! You'll break your hymen and no man will ever marry you—STOP!" Once again, more negative associations with sex: *dirty-perverted-not healthy.*

When Louise came to me as a patient, she explained that sex with her husband was very unsatisfying. She had learned her "no sex" lesson too well. Her husband mounted her with little or no romance or tenderness as foreplay, entered her in the missionary position, almost immediately ejaculated, rolled off and went to sleep. They rarely had sex. He seemed almost apologetic when they did, and it was always very unpleasant for her. She never experienced a sexually loving or intimate moment with him. She was unable to have orgasms with her husband.

She further explained that she had a lover with whom sex was sensual and satisfying. "We play and make love for hours. It feels so good and is such fun. I usually have several orgasms. But, I'm afraid of what would happen if my husband found out. It is his *best* friend. He would be HORRIFIED. I feel *dirty* and *perverted* when I think of what he would say. I'm ashamed."

Louise had put together her mother's message that sexual activity whether alone or with a partner is "dirty, horrifying and perverted." Louise had good feelings about masturbating, but it had to remain hidden so mother wouldn't find out it was a satisfying experience to her. She used mother's established equation:

Sex = dirty = perverted = horrifying when found out.

And she added her own feelings:

Satisfying sex = hiding = sneaking = dishonest = illicit.

Putting her feeling together with mother's association and values, she arrived at her final equation about her own sexual behavior:

Satisfying sex = hiding = illicit = dirty = horrifying (if found out) = FUN = FEELS GOOD.

Therefore, in her marriage no satisfying sex could be allowed according to her mother's formula: sex = dirty. There was nothing dirty about sex in her marriage; it was legal, appropriate, and acceptable. Louise had no childhood association that satisfying sex was appropriate or acceptable behavior. So, in fact, she really couldn't have satisfying, normal, healthy sex with her husband—only the "*dirty sex*" with her lover.

Satisfying sex was related to sneaking, hiding and creating a situation where it would be horrifying for her husband to find out. She was able to set up this situation by having an affair with her husband's best friend. For her husband, finding her in bed with his best friend would be "horrifying."

So you see, in this sense, extra-marital behavior is designed according to childhood orders set down by mother. The young adult incorporates into his sexual practices, the associations and equations dictated to him during his childhood. Essentially, he has been trained for extra-marital sex from his early education by his well-meaning mother.

Extra-marital sex can keep the man a little boy or the woman a little girl. Lying, stealing, cheating, hiding from mommie or daddy, is what little boys and girls do. People who are cheating on their mates are duplicating these childhood behaviors. The married man or woman who is promiscuous may still be hanging on to early childhood behavior.

Extra-marital affairs can also be explained as "insurance policies." "Just in case you leave me by death or for another partner, I'll have someone on the side. They will hug me, kiss me, pet and comfort me. If you die and I have someone else, I won't feel that desperate loneliness. I'll be OK. I'll have somebody to caress me, to love me, to lie with me at night—so I'll survive."

The extra-marital affair can also be understood in another conceptual framework, as a prime vehicle for anger. It is one of the most destructive examples of what I have described earlier as an "instead." The affair can be used as a substitute for anger when one partner is furious and can't express the anger directly.

For example . . . You've embarrassed me in front of our friends, or you insulted me when my parents were over, or you said I made a horrible mistake when I tried so hard to please you.

"Now I don't get furious at you and yell and scream and tell you what's bothering me. 'Instead' of standing up to you, I say to myself, "I'll show him. Tomorrow afternoon, I'm going to be with Henry in a motel and we are going to have wild sex, and I'm going to have glorious orgasms.' " Thus, the extra-marital affair can assuage deep anger, and the cheater may well experience reduced anxiety and temporary relief, until guilt moves in and feelings of inadequacy and worthlessness enter.

But the affair is like a smokescreen. It creates distance and keeps you from seeing what is really happening within your marriage.[1] You're so happy with your lover, that you become blind to *your* role in the pain of your own marriage. It prevents you from looking at *your* part in the problem.

As a psychologist, I neither disapprove nor approve of extra-marital behavior. My concern is with the damage to the character caused by the "unrelenting ego." We have as part of our ego a section which could be called the "Overseer" or "Parent Department." This section is formed very early in our childhood and includes a very strict understanding of right/wrong or appropriate/inappropriate. All our behavior is checked and filed in this department. It is measured by our "unrelenting ego," with its emotional structuring. Typically, the extra-marital partner is actively engaged in lying, manipulating and being deceitful. This is very costly to the core and humanity of the personality. It is as though the ego says to its lying self, "I am NOT willing to tolerate your assault on my integrity. Your lying is destroying my respect for me and my love for me. I'll get you for this when you least expect it. I'll destroy your happy moments, your success—just wait and see." And since we are very self-destructive—the "unrelenting ego" wins and pays us back for these deceptions with feelings of worthlessness, inadequacy and self-hate.

The price of lying is the negative feelings towards ourselves which arise when our "unrelenting ego" gets back at us. It takes too much precious time to be negative to yourself verbally and to feel guilty about how "wrong" you think your illicit behavior may be. This time spent negatively putting yourself down, re-

(1) Edwards, John N., *Extra-Marital Involvement: Fact & Theory,* Journal of Sex Research, 9, No. 3, 1973, p. 215.

duces "life-time" that could be allotted to being creative, inventive and effective. We try to defend against these negative feelings with a Mr. or Mrs. Oom-pa-pa façade, or by being super-critical. We attempt to cover up our self-hate by hiding behind wealth, clothes, possessions and talents. But it really never works with your most important critic and friend—YOU.

I encourage honesty, because it is the easiest, most productive route to a happy life. When your "unrelenting ego" gets off your back, there is an adrenalin-like effect of elation and maximized personal freedom. New possibilities and horizons become available to you. You have time to think and to be productive.

A good marriage is hard work. It takes two active, motivated and honest partners who are willing to share feelings, compromise and talk about what they need and want.

Living with someone you love and respect is an ideal human state, and certainly worth working for. YOU deserve a good marriage with normal, healthy, fun sex. Get to work!

Chapter XI

Fear of Death – The Ultimate Distancer

NOBODY gets out of here alive.

Whether you're the company boss or the new clerk, whether you're surrounded by great wealth or abject poverty, whether you're world renowned or unknown—the end is the same for all of us.

We are all guests in this beautiful world.

If I love you, and am dependent on you, and adore you until I ache, I'm going to *be wiped out* when you die. How will I get through it? What will I do?

So, I'm going to love you just a little—not too much, not too close. I'm going to tell you every week that I hate your hair-style or that you're too fat. This way, when you die—I'll be able to stay alive. I won't hurt so much . . . I won't ache so much . . . I won't feel quite so lonely. I'll be able to say to myself, I didn't love deeply anyway—it's not such a loss.

Whenever my patients give me this kind of message,

I explain that they might as well love each other passionately. Relish in the pleasure you experience with your love. The reality is—whether you love desperately or whether you love only a little, if your lover dies, you *are wiped out*. All any of us have is the now, the *precious now*. Enjoy it!

And it's tough. Who wants to be the one left alone, destroyed, heartbroken—unable to watch lovers holding hands or hear romantic music because it makes you cry and remember? It's all too sad.

Who wants to walk around with part of their insides missing? How do you survive without anyone to share the fun, to laugh with, to smell their skin, or to watch and touch when they're sleeping?

Who wants to create a whole new life when the old one felt just right—when the one you had, although not perfect, was the one you wanted . . . in fact, you never knew how much. How sad it is to remember and realize how good and how sweet your life together was.

Death is like a burglar who comes in the middle of the night and steals your most precious possession. When death leaves, you look around at the mess—the destruction, the loss. You're furious. You've been ROBBED.

You say you're not angry: "How could I be furious that my husband or wife or father or mother or child or friend died? They couldn't help it. They didn't want to die. It seems 'crazy' to be furious."

How do you feel about a thief who comes into your home and steals all your furniture, clothes and beloved mementos from childhood? You *are furious*; you *are angry*. It's understandable that you want to strangle him. And so it is with Death. You're FURIOUS!

Death leaves you feeling helpless and rejected. There's nothing you can do. You could kill your loved one for leaving you, and yet you know it wasn't his fault.

You hate them for making you feel so lonely and

rejected, and yet you realize that they are not to blame.

It is common to have these conflicting normal/crazy feelings about death: I hate them for dying—he or she couldn't help it—I hate them.

ROSE

We are all trained as children to avoid conflicting feelings, so that when they do emerge, we are usually unable to cope with them. We haven't learned the skills to deal with conflicts. We can only incorporate the "nice feelings" our parents will allow; *no anger*, is the rule.

This became apparent when I treated a widow in London, named Rose. She was a healthy, fifty-three-year old active business woman who enjoyed the linen shop she and her husband owned. The two of them were always together either at work or at home. They were happy, busy people. Suddenly, he had a fatal stroke.

"She carried on very little at the funeral" her friends said. "And she never talks about him at all anymore—not since the day he passed on."

It was as though Rose had also died. She closed up the shop, became sullen and morose, stayed at home, wouldn't answer her phone and would rarely see her friends.

Rose's daughter, who was a school teacher, brought her mother to see me. She had heard me lecture at a University conference in Leeds. The daughter was concerned that her mother seemed unable to leave her house since the funeral. "It's as though she's a prisoner in her own home—she never gets out. I'm really worried."

I explained to the daughter, "Your mother has probably become housebound. She may be unable to leave the house because of bottled-up anger feelings for your father which she is unable to express. She may feel that *even thinking* angry thoughts is sick or crazy. She might be afraid to blurt out some of her anger in public. Unconsciously, she may have decided to keep the 'crazy' lady locked up where she couldn't talk to anyone or do any damage."

After only eight sessions with me, Rose snapped back to life, opened her shop, and was the active, "happy old Rose," once more. What was the magic? What happened in the therapy sessions?

Essentially, I helped Rose to get her angry/crazy/conflicting feelings OUT-OF-HER-MOUTH.

On the first session, I talked about how normal it was to be angry with the person who dies. Rose argued with me, "But the poor darling couldn't help it, didn't want it. He loved life. Now that he's gone it would be sacrilegious to be angry with him. I can't."

After our first session, she reported, "I felt like going to the market. I don't know what came over me. It's the first time I've gone shopping since the funeral. I just got up and went."

On the second session, I started demonstrating to Rose what appropriate anger would be, for her to express to her husband. I explained this would be healthy to say even though he was now dead. I acted as Rose's model. I started playing Rose's role by banging my fist against the arm of my chair, and continued banging away as I screamed: "How could you do this to me? I needed you. I loved you. You were the center of my life. My best friend! I hate you for dropping dead! I could kill you! You're awful, cruel. I HATE YOU!"

Rose started crying, "I don't want you to talk like that to him. The poor love never was cruel to me. Never! He was a lamb. It's not right for you to carry on like that with all your screaming Doctor—not right."

Her daughter called me the next day and said she was so pleased. Her mother had asked her out to lunch. "I can't believe how much better she looks already—after only two sessions. It's wonderful."

Rose's parents weren't able to offer her this kind of modeling when she was little, because they couldn't deal with their *own* anger or conflicting feelings. Now in my office, Rose could watch me play-out her role—talking to her dead husband. She could get a first hand view of what to do, in the event she wanted to use me as a model and learn a new way. I showed her a new emotional *route* to *travel*. This was an alternative to locking herself up in her house.

I explained to Rose that I was giving what I felt was appropriate anger to her husband. She could do or say whatever she wanted. She didn't need to do it *my way*—my way was neither "good" nor "bad."

Each time she came to see me, I continued modeling the anger I felt she had submerged. By the sixth session, Rose took over and began yelling at her dead husband herself, holding her fist up in the air. It was after this session that she made arrangements to re-open the store.

Our work was finished soon after Rose was able to get out all her "crazy/normal" feelings: "He couldn't help it . . . I could kill him . . . He couldn't help it . . . I love him . . . I could strangle him for leaving me . . . What a love he was . . . I hate him for leaving me!"

During our sessions, I took Rose by the hand and showed her the way to anger. She trusted me and followed me. Soon she found her own way. Then she was ready and able to carry on with her active life, by herself.

BRAD

There are many ways to avoid facing the painful reality of Death . . . ignoring it is one of the most common ways. Often patients come to me with the conviction that Death has nothing to do with their lives. They feel they will be excluded from the inevitability of death. We can't afford this unrealistic luxury. It's much better to accept the existence of your death—to know it's there waiting for you—so you can make every living moment count.

I'd like to tell you about Brad and how he attempted to block out facing Death.

Brad is a very bald, extremely overweight, talented and successful man of fifty-two. He's Mr. Personality and the executive Vice-President of a major, international company. He's a brilliant force in his industry.

Potentially, Brad has many of the important ingredients for living. But his unconscious terror of his own Death has forced him away from a meaningful life.

Brad came to see me because he was frightened and confused about his frequent depressions. He said to me, "I don't understand. I'm sitting on top of the world. I've got everything. Everyone envies me. Since my divorce, I haven't been alone for a minute. I always have a gorgeous young blonde hanging on my arm. With all I have going for me, why do I feel so lonely and neglected so much of the time?"

Brad is attracted to much younger girls. "Not that I'm a dirty old man or anything," he always jokes. "They're fun. I like girls in their early twenties. I've had many people put me down by saying, 'Why don't you act your own age? Why don't you go out with women who are at least in their late thirties or forties? Are you scared you can only make it with young girls?"

"I don't give a damn what friends say," Brad exclaimed to me. "I love making it with youngees."

I told Brad about other experiences I've had with patients in their forties and fifties who dated or married or had extra-marital affairs with much younger women. In their therapy, we would discuss their fears of dying. When these patients were able to talk or cry about their helplessness in relation to aging and discuss their anger about the inevitability of death, they would assume a more realistic position about the years ahead. For example, a middle-aged patient, age fifty-five, cried to me saying, "It's clear I'm more than half-way through my life. I'm not ready for this! I feel sixteen. But there isn't that much time left. I want to make each moment count. My friends are dropping dead all around me. How much time do I have left?"

Once we are able to deal intensely with their fears of dying, changes occur. These patients start moving toward women who are their intellectual and chronological peers. These are the women with whom the giving-receiving can be the greatest.

We then talked about Brad's fears of aging and dying. "I don't want to deal with death," he said. "Young girls help me forget. When I have this twenty-year old beside me, I can look at her youth, her smooth, tight skin and her thick, lustrous hair, and I feel like I'm her age—almost. When I'm with her, the youth sort of rubs off. It's contagious."

"Nonsense," I interrupted, "you're just kidding yourself and putting on blinders. Besides, you're missing too much. You're doing all the giving. No one is taking care of YOU."

A man needs a truly loving, close relationship, where he can *receive* something for himself as well as give. I think his chances are greater if he is involved with a woman who is similar to him in experience—a woman who is close to him in life-style and life-expectancy. I find that patients, both men and women, who are much older than their mates, tend to be the parent in the relationship. This isn't healthy. Everyone deserves to be babies and cared for some of the time. It is important to be able to feel your own helplessness and "littleness." Always playing the *giver* isn't fair to you.

Older men with a great deal of money, security and/or status are never sure why the young girl wants to be with them. One patient reported that he examined his face daily, praying there wouldn't be any new wrinkles or sagging. He was always worried, "Is she balling some young character when I leave?" Probably.

Have you ever considered the difference in turgidity between the genitals of a twenty-two year old and a fifty-two year old male? The worries the older man lives with daily are very realistic.

The young girl, on the other hand, also pays a tremendous price. Making love to an older man who may be physically unattractive, may work as a deal or trade-off. But there is considerable ego damage in terms of loss of integrity and compromise. I have a young actress as a patient who lives with an older man. She explained: "I feel too lonely and desperate in this town. He gives me television work, security and protection, and I give his ego a boost, because he thinks I'm young and pretty. That's OK with me."

It's a big responsibility for the therapist to take on a patient like this young woman. Because, as she begins to feel better about herself, she won't be able to trade-off or compromise in a relationship. Her dignity and self-worth will become primary considerations. She will look for love instead of security in her lover. This will probably result in her leaving the older man which may mean his stopping support for her career. In this case, if the therapist does a good job, the patient may be out of work! Fortunately, as we feel more self-worth, alternate *routes* to *travel* become available to us. People are able to find their own jobs and create their own security, when they feel good about themselves.

CLAIRE

Here is another example of a young woman living with an older man. When I was working in London, one of my patients, Claire, was a twenty-two-year old student involved in an affair with a forty-five-year old man whom she spoke of as being "very mature and reliable." Her husband had no knowledge of the affair. Claire saw her lover daily.

"He takes care of me," she said gratefully. "He

took me for rides to the country, out to lunch, paid bills for me—even took care of some of my mother's debts. My mother thought he was 'smashing,' even though he was fat and as old as she was. She didn't mind the sneaking about. As long as he took care of me, it was fine with her."

Claire continued, "Even though I love this man in a way because he's so good to me, I can't stand having sex with him. He's so fat that he perspires a good deal. It makes me sick. I can't bear that. I fake my orgasms and he doesn't know it. I dread when he's all wet like that. But I do love the fun we have when we're not in bed. I'd never manage without him. I feel so safe when he's around. He's a love."

After a year of therapy, Claire did leave her lover because lying and "sneaking about" was no longer an acceptable *route* for her.

By being aware of Death, the importance of every single moment is increased. If a middle-aged man fantasizes he's twenty, he can afford to be frivolous about time. When you come to grips with the reality that your life may be two-thirds over, there is increased motivation to live every moment. With a partner who is your peer, you both have the same risks and problems with Death and the same "time-left, time-running-out" responsibility to your Life. Every moment can be appreciated and savored.

MARSHA AND JEREMY

What do you do when you think your wife is going to die? How do you cope with this kind of reality? I want to look at how Marsha and Jeremy dealt with the problem.

Marsha and Jeremy, a couple in their early forties, were my patients. They originally came to see me because they were having sexual problems. Marsha had a mastectomy. Because she felt disfigured, she assumed her husband would be repelled by the sight of her body. To avoid this imagined rejection, she withdrew from having any sexual activity.

Part of this couple's problem was that Jeremy was unable to express feelings. We worked on this for several weeks. Jeremy truly loved Marsha and found her beautiful and sexually stimulating both before and after her surgery. As I continued working with Jeremy, he became better able to express his feelings and reassure Marsha of his love and interest. Because he was sincerely able to tell her how desirable she was for him, Marsha became more relaxed and they moved into the kind of playful, warm and passionate sex they both enjoyed before her operation.

It had been almost two years since they discovered that Marsha had breast cancer. They thought they were finished with that problem when—WHAM—Marsha was in the hospital again. Cancer had returned. This time her other breast was removed. For five days after the surgery, they were concerned about her dying. She finally rallied and made a remarkable post-operative recovery. Marsha's bout with death was almost more than Jeremy could handle. He was overcome with fear. He wanted to protect himself from the pain of losing Marsha. This close contact with death put an unbearable strain on the marriage. His fear almost paralyzed any interaction between them.

Marsha felt that because she almost died, Jeremy didn't want to get near her.

They came to me to discuss their problem.

Marsha was in tears explaining that they really hadn't been able to get close again since her operation. She felt terribly alone.

While Marsha was sobbing, Jeremy was calmly pointing out that he was under a lot of pressures at the office. He discussed his work with the emotional involvement you might expect from someone reviewing a grocery list.

I stopped him. I was angry with him. "Jeremy," I

said, "I can't stand your deadness. You're like a corpse! Your wife, your love, is playing Russian Roulette with cancer. She almost died. I don't want you to talk about business!" Then I felt more tender toward Jeremy and said, "My hunch is you're too frightened to express any anger, so you're talking in your dead-pan style about work. I understand, and I know you love Marsha. For five days you weren't sure whether or not she was going to survive. You told me how terrified you were. I would like you to try to get in touch with these frightening feelings. This lady you love almost left you by dying!

"You knew she couldn't help it and didn't want to have anything wrong with her body. She didn't want to die. Yet you're still stuck with your fury. She'll feel less guilty if you can give her your anger."

I modeled for Jeremy and took his role as I yelled at Marsha. "Damn you for having cancer and almost dying on me! I hate you. I could kill you! Twice you've pulled this horror on me. I hate it. Why me? I feel cheated. I love you. I don't want you to do this to me. I hate this. I don't want to LOSE you!"

Marsha was crying. "My God! It's a relief to hear you say that. I feel guilty, and I do feel cheated. Why me? I'm angry too! I've been afraid to bring it up, but it's such a relief to hear you talk about it now."

"Marsha, I never dreamed you'd want me to say that," Jeremy said, looking shocked. "And Doctor Kassorla, I have been thinking about every word you've just said. I felt I was a horrible person for even harboring such thoughts."

"Not horrible Jeremy," I said. "Just normal and human. You have *both* been cheated. You *are* in a frightening place. At least, if all the anger and negative feelings you have can surface, you will be able to get them *out-of-your-mouths* and out of the way. Then, you'll have more time for your good, close, loving feelings to emerge. There's room in your emotional house for only one strong feeling at a time. It's not possible to get close and enjoy your time together when you're both so furious. It's good to get your anger out."

I told Jeremy that he had made the initial error of falling in love with a human being, a mortal. "In any love situation, one of the partners will die first. It would be nice if a couple could live to old age together. But I want you to face this—your wife almost left you and she may do it again. Only this time, it may be fatal. You have a right to be furious. Who else are you going to find? There are only other human beings out there. Everybody is mortal. All of us are caught in the same human trap—we are all dying."

Jeremy responded by saying that he still felt it was easier to stay away from feelings—to talk about business or anything. "If I can build walls around myself, neither Marsha nor anyone else can ever hurt me. I'll be better off isolated from all this emotional stuff. My 'dead-pan,' as you call it, protects me. It's like novacaine, it keeps the pain away."

"Nonsense!" I interrupted. "You can't deny this pain. It's all over both of you. My hunch is you're thinking about it constantly." They were nodding their heads affirmatively. "Get it out! Finish with it. YOU HAVE TIME NOW. Take it. Grab it!"

Marsha was confused. "I don't know how to get through his walls."

"BANG THEM DOWN!" I screamed. "Tell him you love him. Get physically close. If he moves away, get closer. Don't listen to him. Hold on!

"Tell him you have today. Who do you know that can swear with any validity that they are going to be alive tomorrow? Jeremy is acting as if he has some sort of guarantee. Nonsense! No one has a guarantee. We're all dying!

"Enjoy the *precious moment*. Enjoy *today*! Otherwise you are both already dead."

I told them that if they loved each other they had time—a week, a month, years—who knows? But if they built walls, they wouldn't have a minute; they didn't have a chance; they'd miss everything.

CHRIS AND KITTY

Kitty died last week.

It was a crazy, unbelievable tragedy. Kitty was thirty-two, a beautiful mother of two boys. She loved to dance, was very athletic, swam, played golf and tennis and had a great sense of humor. Everybody loved Kitty. She was always the center of attention at a party because she was so easy to be with.

Chris and Kitty, along with their two children, were in Hawaii on a vacation. In the morning she played golf and later swam with the children. After a lovely tropical lunch, she went to take a rest and—BOOM—she dropped dead! It was such a horrible, freakish blow.

It was a great shock to Chris, suddenly a widower with two children at the age of thirty-three.

People handled the shock in different ways.

As I've said before, the healthiest way to cope with death is anger, actually rage. Loved ones who are left behind experience tremendous rage and helplessness. Nothing anyone can do will bring the person you lost back to you again. The feelings of helplessness can in some ways be lessened by keeping friends near you and talking to them about the way you feel.

And what do you say when you meet the widower or the widow.

I went over to the house as soon as I heard Chris was back. I hugged him and held him. I hung on to him for a long time. We just sort of rocked back and forth. He sat down on the floor and I sat beside him. I didn't say anything, just held his hand.

Many of his friends explained they were very uncomfortable about going to see Chris. The major fears expressed were, "What should I do? What should I say?"

The whole point is that you don't have to say anything. Just bring your body close. Hold their hands and be quiet. That is the way to help the bereaved person. If they want to talk, fine. You're their friend; share your honest feelings with them. I feel the best comfort is to have warm bodies of people who care, close about you, holding on to you.

A few of Chris's friends told me privately they felt guilty. They had some hidden feelings which they couldn't express, such as, "Thank God it isn't my wife; thank God it isn't the woman I love; thank God it's Kitty and not me." They felt ashamed because they harbored these thoughts.

"These are very normal feelings," I suggested. "It's very understandable when you are at a funeral to say to yourself, 'Thank God, that isn't me, my mother or my sister or my father or my best friend!' Yet, most people feel desperately guilty about having these feelings."

While I would never suggest that anyone say this to the mourner, I do suggest that they at least realize it is normal and that everybody has these thoughts at the time of death.

If we live long enough, we see most of the people we love die. "What is important in this life? What's it all about?" These are the questions I hear my patients asking themselves . . . and me.

Spend today well. Fill it with loving your family, your friends and yourself. Work at what you feel is worthwhile; become involved in the welfare of your community; enjoy your body and your mind. That's what it's all about.

All any of us have is the moment . . .

Enjoy this moment . . . NOW.

There is a fear we learn very early in life—that good things must end. This is a fear I have heard expressed all over the world.

While attending a party in Spain, a beautiful child

came up to me. I said, "My what a gorgeous little girl." The grandmother, who was sitting next to me, started spitting to the side. I asked a friend why she was spitting. He explained that she was warding off evil spirits. I had said something good, and since the grandmother's superstition suggested that bad comes after good, she was pushing away the bad by spitting. This had become an automatic gesture for the old woman.

Jewish people have a term, *einahora,* or *kein an einahora*, which means essentially no evil spirit or damage should come to you. It is similar to the Spanish concept of warding off evil spirits and it is expressed after a great compliment. For example, if this same pretty child approached me in a Jewish home and I said, "What a gorgeous little girl," it is very likely that one of the older people would respond with, "Kein an einahora," or no evil spirit should hurt the child.

In Greek mythology there is a word "hubris," which suggests it would be wise to offer some tribute, acknowledgment or pay-off with "due regard for the Gods" following good fortune or a great compliment. If not, it is believed you run the risk of losing it.

In American life, we often hear the phrase "knock on wood." It is the same fear—warding off evil spirits after something good happens or is expressed.

We are so imbued with this fear of evil following good, that when we do get into a pleasant situation, we unconsciously try to stop it by introducing something to end it.

It's as if every relationship has to have an ongoing tragedy. If things are too good we think, "Heaven forbid, one of us must introduce the calamity before the Gods do." This is nonsense!

Words such as "if" and "when" can also destroy the *precious moment*. For example, when we are enjoying a lovely dinner, I might say, "*If only* . . . I had worn my green dress. *If only* . . . we had gone to

Chasen's. *If only* . . . Jackie and Ronnie had been able to come with us." The "if onlys" inevitably diminish the pleasure. Some people also use "whens" . . . *When* we're older we'll have more money, and we'll go on that holiday . . . *When* the children are grown, we'll . . . *When* the car is paid off, we'll . . . *When* summer comes, we'll . . . etc."

They also miss the *precious NOW moment.*

It is a tragedy that most of us are not enjoying ourselves when we ARE alive. Because of our negative life-styles and the ways we stop the pleasure, we experience very little pure happiness during our life-times. If we are lucky, before we die, we may have truly relished and experienced only a few years of satisfying living because of our "if onlys, whens, and knock-on-woods." Those missed moments can never be relived.

Although it is very difficult, I encourage people to attempt to *stay* with the precious moment when they are feeling close, loving and good about themselves. When you feel this way you may even become aware of some anxiety or fear. If you do get in touch with these feelings, good! *Give-yourself-a-kiss* and try to hang-in there a little longer. STRETCH IT OUT FOR FIVE MINUTES MORE.

Try to *extend* the moment. If you stretch the moment five minutes today, maybe you can have six minutes of pleasure tomorrow and seven more minutes the next day. GOOD! ENJOY YOUR PRECIOUS LIFE!

Chapter XII

Divorce: A Waste of Time

Either your or your next door neighbor is likely to get a divorce this year! This has now become a shocking reality. Since 1910, the divorce rate in this country has increased almost 1000%. People are marrying, divorcing, marrying and getting divorced again! The United States Census Bureau stated in 1971 that the annual number of divorces in the preceding ten year period rose by 80%. In 1973, it was estimated that the divorce rate for the nation was half as great as marriages for that year. In California, the estimate was even higher and more staggering, 60%.

Considering these facts and figures, and because in my work I have found that most marriages are repairable, with few exceptions my conclusion is that DIVORCE IS A WASTE OF TIME!

When couples come to me with marital problems, even when the negatives seem unbearable, I suggest they delay any divorce plans. I recommend that they come into therapy and make a six-month commitment to work on the marriage with no further talk of divorce during this period. I usually explain that if their marriage was worth going into originally, they deserve the opportunity to examine the problems of their relationship one more time, in a therapeutic setting. Hopefully, during this time, they will be able to take a more realistic look at how they are each contributing to the destruction of the marriage. Otherwise, I predict they will move into the divorced world and find a similar partner with a different body and different head and find themselves in the "marriage-go-round" cycle again.

Their second or third or fourth partner may be taller, shorter, fatter, thinner, older, richer or more educated . . . but the result is the same. We keep re-playing the same old unhappiness records we learned in childhood. And for what? If we marry a dozen times, we'll find our psychologically similar partner (i.e. mother) each time. That's all there is . . . our "gears" have been set in childhood. We continue to fall in love with the same kind of personality whose "gear-teeth" will mesh with ours. The psychological matching is similar with every appealing prospective partner. Suddenly, after we're well into the next marriage, we come to the realization, "I've done it again! I've ended up with the same feelings about myself that I had in the last marriage. I feel awful . . . I'm unhappy. I can't believe I've done it again!"

In this marriage-go-round, we do end up, essentially, with the same feelings and the same partner. If there were problems in marriage #1, and you haven't changed markedly, you will pick a similar partner for marriage #2. Unless there has been an important therapeutic intervention and resulting personality change, we bring our old childhood packages with our old styles, into the new marriage. We have to change ourselves before we can expect the new relationship to be any different than our discard. If you have not changed, the prediction seems obvious and very sad . . . another divorce.

Who can afford the cost of divorce in terms of the loss in energy and stability, the guilt and the pain? Divorce is surrounded by loneliness and confusion; families are torn apart and children are splattered emotionally against the walls. The psychological readjustment for everyone is traumatic; the drastically modified life-style is devastating. It is important to create a solid base and find stability in your life. There is too little security in the marriage/divorce hysteria—roots are cut very deeply. People feel frightened and unsafe. The single world is full of repeaters, and there is a tragic inevitability about our going back to the same types.

Because I believe we do it over and over again, it seems to make sense to stay in the relationship and ask ourselves: "Why do I need to be unhappy in my marriage. Why do I find it so difficult to get close. How do I set up the pain? I have to work on *me* before we can work on *us*."

And how do you work on YOU? It is essential for you to take the responsibility for the problems in your marriage. Look at how you are setting up the uncomfortable feelings and arguments. When I say this to a new patient, the immediate reaction is "I'm not going to be the fall guy. There are two of us making the marriage a mess, not just me. I'm not taking the blame —not me, Doctor. I've put everything I have into this marriage. And he (or she) doesn't appreciate how I've sacrificed—how considerate I've been. Anyway, it's all his fault. He is so unreasonable. He is so selfish. He's impossible. Who could live with a . . . etc."

Progress begins when each partner is finally able to say, "There are two of us creating *our* problems and I want to examine *my* part." In a court of law you might hear a judge say, "You're 50% to blame and your mate is 50% to blame." In therapy, I encourage my patients to throw away blame. It is not possible to create changes in the marriage when everything is clouded by blame. If your goal is to place blame on your mate, you can always find a friend who will listen sympathetically and judge your behavior as "right" and your partner's as "wrong." Then you'll be off the hook with only part of the responsibility, part of the guilt, part of the blame. But I'd like both partners to throw away right, wrong, guilt, fault, and most important—throw out blame. These words blind you from SEEING your role in the problem. Focusing on your partner's errors blurs the problems and pushes away the possibility of change.

As children, we learn that blaming the other fellow works in helping us to avoid punishment. For example, you are three years old and have just spilled your finger paints on the floor. If you can blame it on the cat, or your brother, then your mother won't have that angry expression on her face that is so frightening to you. However, the major problem with blame is that it prevents learning. You won't be able to understand what you did to cause the spill nor will you know how to avoid repeating the experience in the future. Instead, your time has been spent pushing the responsibility on the cat. It makes sense to blame someone else when you are little; then you don't get that spanking or scolding. Mother is your world and you want to keep her smiling at you. That means everything to you when you are small.

The problem with using blame as an adult goal is that it precludes change. If your goal picture includes working for a happier marriage . . . stop the blaming!

One of the most common vehicles used in problem marriages is blaming. I find that couples who are considering divorce use a great deal of blame in their verbal messages. I call this kind of killer message, "divorce talk."

Here are some examples: "I'm not getting enough out of this marriage because you are so mean . . . you're always criticizing me . . . you never want to go out with me . . . you never kiss me . . . you never talk to me . . . you're having an affair with our television set . . . you never remember my . . . etc."

Stop the blaming! Stop the divorce talk.

You are creating your part in the problem. Try to take a look and *see*. If you aren't getting affectionate embraces, somehow you're stopping it. Divorce talk and blaming are "insteads" that will keep you too busy to examine your own behavior. If you can stop these "insteads," you may be able to come up with some of the reasons you are setting up the loneliness and distancing in your marriage.

If your goal is to improve the marriage, concentrate your energies on your role in the relationship. Investigate how you are contributing to the problem. Give yourself positives and kisses. You're *seeing*. Good.

Here is a case history that will help you to understand how blaming your partner will prevent you from seeing your own behavior and from getting what you want in your marriage.

STU AND SHERYLL

Sheryll first came to see me alone. She didn't want to work on the marriage problems with her husband, Stu. She wanted a divorce. Her complaints included, "He's so cold. He rarely touches me, except during intercourse. I'm jealous everytime I see a man and woman hugging and kissing. Why doesn't he act like that with me? He just can't be demonstrative. No matter how much I beg or plead for a show of affection, I get nothing . . . nothing. When I was single, I loved being with attentive men. I don't know how I got into this marriage with such a cold fish!"

"Sheryll," I said, "My patients often talk about being able to get close and be affectionate when they're dating. There is considerable 'built-in' distance in a dating situation. When you are seeing a man occasionally, you're not very involved and there is a good deal of space. Your fears about getting too close won't start operating."

"What makes you think I can't get close, Doctor?" Sheryll said, "I love being close, I love it."

"Sheryll," I said, "I hear you, and I know you are consciously telling me the truth. I believe you, and I realize you believe what you're saying. You *think* you want a warm and loving man around. However, as we get into our work together, you'll probably find that what's really happening is that *you* sabotage the affection . . . you're too frightened to get close."

"Me!" Sheryll said, astonished. "Never! I know how to get close. It's Stu's problem, not mine. I can just see myself single, dating affectionate men, having exciting times. It would be such fun! I could get a marvelous job and be with brilliant people all day."

"Sheryll," I said, "I had another patient who I'll call Jenny. She was similar to you in many ways. She had four children and no job skills or training. Jenny had little understanding of what was out there in the single world. She was unwilling to work on her marriage problems, and she quit therapy. Jenny thought that all she had to do was get a divorce, and she'd 'knock them dead.' The single world was very lonely and disappointing for her. And as for her marvelous job—she ended up with varicose veins selling brassieres at the May Company!

"Now, it may be that divorce is recommended in your marriage," I continued. "If it is, we'll go to work on that. I'm interested in helping you get what *you* want. For a short period of time, if that's agreeable to you, I would like to take a look at your interactions in the marriage. If you are willing to make this limited commitment, we can examine how you might be sabotaging the closeness in your relationship with Stu.

"When working with other patients, I find that they nag their partners for the very gestures and behaviors they believe they want but are afraid to receive. In your case, you might nag and say, 'Why aren't you more affectionate? Why don't you put your arms around me? Why . . . etc! If you *are* afraid of Stu's being affectionate with you . . . your nagging message would keep him away from you. Nagging causes the *reverse* of what you want to happen, and nagging causes distance."

After working with Sheryll for several weeks, she was willing to look at the possibility that she was involved in helping to create the problems in her marriage. She agreed to postpone her plans for divorce, and she asked Stu to work with her in one of my couples groups. He thought this would be a fine idea.

On their fourth group session together, Sheryll started her old blaming messages, "How come you never kiss me when we're with people? I wish you'd come over to where I'm sitting and kiss me when you arrive late to group. I haven't seen you all day. I hate driving here alone to meet you. At least you could give me a little kiss when you come in the room. It wouldn't hurt you. You always just walk in and sit down without even a hello. I feel like you don't even know me or see me."

Stu replied, "Honey, I feel awkward about walking over to kiss you in front of everyone. I guess I'm a little conservative. Actually, I always thought it would make you uncomfortable too, so I've deliberately avoided kissing you when we meet. I'm sorry. I'm not sure I would feel natural kissing you in public even though I like to please you."

Sheryll said curtly, "Don't do me any favors, Stu. Don't 'please' me. I'm not looking for charity, you know. If you don't feel good about kissing me, forget it!"

"Hold on," I interjected. "I want to try something. I'd like you to practice a new behavior with me. I think affection is difficult for you. I believe you're both uncomfortable about getting close."

I asked them if they were willing to work on this

"kissing" problem, and they agreed. We all sat down next to each other. I was on one side of Sheryll and Stu was on the other. I held Sheryll's hand and suggested she tell Stu directly and without nagging what she wanted. Earlier, it was easy for her to complain to him when he was across the room. Now that he was sitting beside her, she had difficulty telling him directly. She was more comfortable with nagging and complaining.

"Give him your 'I want' Sheryll," I suggested. "Try it now. Look at him and tell him you want a kiss."

Sheryll became flushed. "This seems so silly," she laughed. "I can't do it. I feel ridiculous."

"You're probably laughing because you're frightened, Sheryll," I said. "Try saying, 'I want a kiss.' "

Again she laughed and was unable to say anything. She kept her eyes down looking into her lap. I put my arm around her, and I continued holding her hand as well. Her body became wet with perspiration.

"Try, Sheryll," I said. "Try to say 'I want a kiss.' I know how difficult this is for you."

"I'm afraid to," she said. Sheryll started crying.

"Try to repeat the words after me," I said. I went slowly, one word at a time. After several minutes she was finally able to say the words to Stu—all of them: "I want a kiss."

Stu responded by leaning toward her cheek to kiss her, and she instantly pulled her head back away from him before he could reach her. Then he quickly moved his body away from her. He looked confused.

Sheryll said, "See, I ask him for a kiss and he pulls away from me. I'm not complaining for nothing, you know. I don't know why I even bother; he . . . etc."

"Sheryll, you pulled away first!" I said. "Stu reached forward to kiss you, and you turned your head away from him."

"I can't believe that—he did it first," Sheryll said.

I knew Sheryll was telling the truth as she experienced it. Her reality was different than the group because her behavior was unconscious. She had no idea she pulled away first. All she experienced was Stu moving back, away from her. The group chimed in loudly reassuring Sheryll she had moved away from Stu first. This was difficult for Sheryll to believe. For the first time in her marriage, she had a chance to *see* what she was doing on a conscious level.

The point is, when Sheryll was complaining and blaming Stu with her divorce talk, "You never kiss me," she was unable to see how she stopped the kiss and the affection. She was unable to understand her responsibility in creating the problems of the marriage.

I find I can help couples work on the marriage when they substitute responsibility, for blame. If you are willing to try this method of working, each partner will assume the following kind of thinking:

> "My partner is fine. How did *I* set up the problems? Where is *my* responsibility in these unpleasant interactions? What am *I* doing to increase the pain? How did *I* stop the fun we were having?"

It will be very difficult for you to ask yourself these questions. However, when you are able to look at yourself, change can begin.

Helping a new patient to look at his responsibility for the pain in the marriage takes time. Just the word "responsibility" often has negative connotations. Our childhood memories are filled with negative equations regarding responsibility which include words like "naughty, guilty" and "you've made a mistake." Throw these negatives away.

I'd like to introduce an adult equation that associates maturity and change with responsibility:

Responsibility = adult behavior = maturity = willingness to SEE = change.

When you can see yourself operating in your old "stop-the-joy-in-the-marriage" style, and when you can *see* your part in the problem, remember to give yourself a kiss. If you can actually *see* yourself doing this, and deliver your kiss to you, then you can start changing. There is hope for the marriage.

Here is an example of what I mean: Your husband (or wife) has asked you not to discuss dieting when you're out socially. He's overweight and is ashamed of his appearance. He's embarrassed about his inability to stick to the diet his Doctor prescribed. He's having a hard enough time trying to abstain from overeating without dealing with any criticism in front of your friends. When they know he's dieting, they seem to continually urge him to taste just another little bite of what they've ordered.

While you are out to dinner with your friends one evening at an Italian restaurant, your husband orders fettucini as his entree and spaghetti for a starter. You want to be helpful so you say, "Oh, darling, that can't be on your diet, that's loaded with calories. It's all pasta and doughie." His face gets red; he gives you a hurt and disgusted look and doesn't talk to you for the rest of the evening. He feels humiliated, and furious with you. The evening is ruined.

Before your remark, you were holding hands and he was affectionate and loving. You were both having such fun. Then your "helpful" comment . . . and the *precious moment* stopped. Your embarrassing remark caused immediate distance between you. The atmosphere was contaminated with negative feelings . . . the joy stopped.

Using your old blaming style, you could focus on him and say: "Oh, he's so sensitive, I can never open my mouth to say anything constructive. He can't take it. He's so touchy. I was only trying to help. If I don't watch him, he won't lose an ounce. I was only thinking of his health. He never appreciates me . . . he never . . . etc."

Keeping your thinking on him stops *your* growth. Look at yourself. Look at how you stopped the pleasure. Stay out of his plate!

If you can take the responsibility and perhaps say, "Maybe I became anxious when everything was so wonderful at the restaurant. Maybe I don't have much room or experience in my life-style patterns for pleasure" . . . then there is hope for the marriage. And more important, there is hope that you will be able to stretch the *precious moment* and have more fun next time. Be willing to kiss yourself for seeing that pleasure is frightening for you, and that *you* sabotaged the fun.

Patients are extremely hard on themselves when they first discover they destroyed the good feelings of the moment. But if your new goal of abandoning blame and looking for the responsibility is to work in creating change, you'll need to be kind to *you*. Stop kicking yourself. Rather, try to uncover new information about yourself that can benefit the relationship. It would be unfair of you to punish yourself for using methods that you thought were sensible when you were two years old. Your reasoning was fine at two—it helped you then. It is understandable that you'd employ these methods now, since we automatically use our early styles. However, as an adult, you can consciously introduce new methods. Risk trying to change. You can put aside your old blaming techniques for something healthier. Taking the responsibility will allow you to strengthen your marriage and move away from divorce.

Perhaps the next time you and your husband are having fun, you can say to yourself, "Watch it, dear human, all this pleasure is a spooky place for you. You're having fun, and your early experiences with good feelings are very limited. Getting close is frightening for you! Try to stay with the good feelings. Stretch them out a bit more. No sabotage please. Don't stop the fun. Just try a few minutes more."

Share with your mate and tell him when you see your part of the responsibility. Then he (or she) may be able to emulate or model your behavior and take the responsibility for himself when the next problem occurs. This will afford you the ideal situation: both of you working on your role in the difficulties of the marriage, both of you taking the responsibility for your behavior, and both of you giving yourselves kisses when you can see how you have set up the problem. Together you can provide these necessary ingredients for a "good" relationship.

As a therapist, I'm sad to see so many couples shuffling their lives around unnecessarily and getting divorced. Eventually, they replay the same old record with new marriage partners. Problems in marriage are never his or hers, but *ours*. A good marriage is hard work and requires constant compromising. There are no villains in the relationship, just two humans, carrying their childhood life-style packages along, hoping for happiness.

A marriage worth going into, is worth trying to save. Get to work! DIVORCE—IS A WASTE OF TIME.

Chapter XIII

Marriage Can Be An Ideal Human State

Having a hand to grasp when you're frightened and need to reach out . . . having someone to hold you and say, "I understand" when everything goes wrong . . . having someone who cares when you're feeling sick . . . having someone to share your problems, who wants to protect you and keep you safe . . . having someone to share your little moments of joy and beauty that no one else could understand . . . having someone you love, loving you . . .

I believe marriage can be an ideal human state. It requires delicate handling and attention. And even more, it requires constant work and genuine concern, much the way a successful business does. In a good marriage, you feel the emotional investments that you're making in each other today, will grow in meaning and richness tomorrow.

Partners in a successful marriage continually need to re-examine their established ways of interacting. All marriages have problems. In a good marriage, both partners work on these problems. It is important that a marriage allow for flexibility, discussion and the airing of differences. For a marriage to survive, both partners need to make compromises and changes, because no matter how great your love, if you are going to be married to a HUMAN, you are going to have problems.

Many misunderstandings will occur because your human, mortal mate will unintentionally hurt your feelings. And the reverse will be true—you will unwittingly hurt his (or her) feelings. No one is that tuned in or aware of how they are communicating. Perhaps, if you could find a computer to fall in love with, the computer would be totally sensitive, all-knowing and wise enough to understand you, your hopes, your thoughts, your needs . . . all the time. A human won't make it. That's the trouble. But it's *good* trouble. Who wants to come home and make love to a computer? How good it feels when you are able to talk to your precious, human partner. You can tell him when your feelings have been wounded. But keep in mind that deep inside, he too, is very little and so easily hurt.

If two people are going to be living together, there will be differences. Differences are fine. However, for the marriage to grow, it is important for the couple to learn to compromise when these differences do occur.

For example: your husband wants to spend your ten-day holiday camping out in the woods with you and the children. He feels roughing it and cooking fresh trout over an open fire every night would be fun. He sees himself smoking his pipe, relaxing, fishing in the lake and enjoying the fresh air. He loves getting away from the noise of the city and can hardly wait to share nature with his family. You hate camping! All this "out-door-sy" talk makes you sick to your stomach. You envision being devoured by mosquitoes, bored to death by the silence of the woods, and repelled by the lack of sanitary facilities. You despise the smell of fish; you don't want to cook and clean up on your holiday, and you abhor the idea of being isolated for ten long days with your four screaming children yelling, "Mommie, what can I do now?" and "Mommie, please let me take this snake home."

Your idea of a ten-day holiday is checking into a luxury hotel by the sea—romantic, candlelight dinners served on white linens with violins in the background—extravagant boutiques close by where you can shop for hours—and, your children no less than two hundred miles away!

Neither one of you is willing to go along with the other's idea of a holiday.

So what do you do now? You compromise! He gets a five-day holiday camping trip with you, the snakes and the children; and you get your luxury holiday, alone with your husband for five glorious days. No one sacrifices!

If he sacrifices and does everything your way, you'll become the child in the relationship, full of guilt and self-hate. Conversely, if you do it all his way, you'll despise him and find a way to retaliate later. When sacrificing, you both lose. While it may feel uncomfortable when you're trying to arrive at a solution that is equitable for both of you, the least costly route in the long run is to compromise.

If either of you had gotten your own way completely for ten days, it would have created an impossible atmosphere filled with hate, resentment and loss of love feelings for each other. Instead of the holiday being an enjoyable time together, it would have served to create distance.

It is critical for each partner to contribute to the fun during his five days of the compromise. Once you have made your deal, enter it with smiles and positives—

no negatives, no complaints. Remember, you're mortal dear humans. Can you afford to throw away five days of living by being negative and focusing on what you *don't* like? Find something that's pleasurable that you *do* like during your period of compromising. Grab every *precious moment* you can . . . ALL the five days, five hours, five minutes . . . enjoy it all with your love.

Through compromising, couples can learn to allow new ideas to enter their thinking. This allows each of them to become re-educated and increase their understanding of their partner's feelings. This is another way change can occur. It is important to be able to continually expand the marriage framework so that it includes new values and behaviors which are agreed to by *both* partners.

It is unfortunate that the idea of change is so frightening to most couples. They fear change will result in the destruction of their marriage. In fact, I find the reverse to be true. Healthy changes can keep a marriage strong and vital. Patients who come to me saying they want out of the marriage are typically dissatisfied with their partner's inability to change. They discuss feeling trapped. Repairing the relationship usually requires making changes in their existing life-styles, allowing for more differences in behavior and freedom in thinking.

The issue of freedom in a marriage is a common concern for many couples. Often one or both of the partners complain that their freedom is curtailed, and that they are too limited in their activities. They want more space. When we start discussing their feelings about freedom, we come to this basic question: what is freedom? From a psychological point of view, freedom is having the choice of deciding where you want to be limited! You can *choose* whatever is important in your life, where you want to be, and what you want to do, your work, your mate, your friends, your political involvements, your city, etc. You will be faced with emotional, psychological, and/or physical limits in all of these situations and places. For example, if you marry a traveling salesman, you are *limited* to the amount of time you can spend together; if you take that pottery class you love, you're *limited* to the number of sessions you can work as you have neither a wheel nor a kiln at home; if you choose to make a specific political commitment you are *limited* to being represented by the candidates of your party's choice. Wherever you go you will find limits. There will be rules to follow, boundaries to respect, manners and rituals to consider.

You can decide whether or not you want to marry a traveling salesman and be limited by his hours away from home, you can decide if that pottery class is limiting because it offers you too little time to be creative; you can decide which political camp you want to join and in either place you will be *limited*.

Freedom = deciding where you will be limited.

Often couples who are contemplating divorce complain they have too little freedom in the marriage. They cry out for more space, more distance.

One of my major efforts as a psychologist has been to cut down on distancing and bring people closer together. I want to point out, however, that some healthy distancing in a relationship may be necessary and recommendable. I've emphasized the word healthy because in many of the chapters, I've talked about the destructive ways people create distance in their lives and unintentionally move away from the people they love. I've described the painful or emotionally unhealthy distancers people use, such as killer talk, insteads, frigidity, extra-marital behavior, etc. These are all damaging to your unrelenting ego and to *you*. However, if couples do require some space and privacy from their mates, it is important for them to talk about this openly, to attempt to get their distance in a more healthy and non-destructive manner. Each partner needs to state what he wants, hopes for and requires in the marriage. After a considerable amount of work in therapy, involving how to share feelings, the couple might then be able to modify, shift and compromise their thinking. This process continues until *both* partners find an arrangement that is workable and mutually satisfying.

ALEX AND MAE

Here is a case which points up the need for some freedom or healthy distance which can exist in a good marriage. Alex and Mae have been married for eighteen years. They both want to enjoy their marriage more and are working together in one of my evening "couples" groups. During one session, Alex told his group that he and Mae were arguing after dinner one evening.

"It was about a film we had seen over the weekend," Alex said. "Funny thing, I couldn't care less about the discussion we had concerning the real meaning of that movie. Yet, during our fight, I was arguing vehemently with Mae about one scene in the film. It seemed so important to me, that I suddenly found myself screaming! I threw my napkin down on my plate and stormed out of the room. I grabbed my car keys and started walking out the front door. Mae tried to stop me. She took hold of my arm and said, 'Where are you going?' I jerked away from her and yelled, 'Out for a breath of air. I can't stand your stupid comments. What do you know about real drama? You missed the whole point of the movie. You make me sick. I'm getting out of here. Just leave me alone!'

"I went to a local film and came home about midnight," Alex said. "It felt great being alone, but I also felt guilty. You know, I must have just wanted a couple of hours by myself, but I was afraid to ask Mae. I was certain she'd say no. Maybe that's why I started the fight."

Mae broke in, "Alex, I don't see anything wrong with your going out for an evening without me. I wanted to set my hair that night anyway. I'm always afraid you'll complain about the curlers looking so messy. I was relieved when you left, and I had some time to myself."

"That's good work, Mae," I said. "Tonight you have both mentioned wanting some distance—some time away from each other. That's normal in a good marriage. And you can have it without the fighting and the petty bickering. I do think that people need some distance from their lovers. Most of my patients report they want to be alone some of the time.

"You can have some recreations or hobbies away from home and each other and still maintain a close and loving relationship. Take some territory for yourself, some emotional space. Your outside activities need to be enjoyable only to *you*, something you value as meaningful. No one else has to agree or approve. You need to find interests that are rewarding for you without threatening the important people in your life. It doesn't have to benefit your family, children, friends, neighbors or your mate. Do something just for *you*.

"Alex, you and Mae can explore this concept of emotional and physical space even further. Together, you can plan the time you may need, or want, to be apart. The space you grabbed the other night with your fighting is too costly, too filled with guilt. Because you love and trust each other and have both made a sexual commitment, you can afford some healthy distancing."

Each couple can decide just how much distancing or time away from each other is comfortable and compatible with their particular needs and limits. No amount of space is right or wrong. The two partners need to work together towards some kind of agreement.

I'm usually amazed when couples boast in social settings that they do "everything" together. Later, when they are alone with me during their therapy sessions, they talk about feeling suffocated by their life-styles, and complain that they long for freedom. I encourage my patients to have some time away from their mates and families. It isn't necessary for couples to share interests in all the same things. You can go to that class in Current Political Issues, and your mate doesn't need to enjoy discussing politics. He may want to take that class in Modern Art which you refer to as globs of unrelated forms and colors. It's fine to have different interests. You can be apart some of the time. You want to play bridge. Good. Your mate hates bridge. He can't remember a single card and doesn't enjoy the game. Go alone. You want to attend that real estate class, and he said he's not interested. Go by yourself. Do some things without each other while feeling safe with your relationship and good about yourselves. Tell him you love and need him. Tell him he's the center of your love world. When you feel secure in your loving, you can be different from your mate, have different ideas, and different preferences. *Different is fine*. Your way is different than his (or hers) and *you're both fine.*

Marriage can be the ideal way for people to live. It's heaven to have your mate close by, working through problems together, helping you with your fears and pain, sharing the fun. There is less mental illness with married couples than with single people. I believe this is because it feels so good, so safe to have a partner to share your life and love.

A good marriage is constant hard work, and it's worth it. Talk to each other, share both anger and love; share your fears and feelings.

MARRIAGE CAN BE AN IDEAL HUMAN STATE!

Chapter XIV

Success

If suddenly a Genie appeared and offered to grant you three wishes—probably one of your wishes would be for success. Most of us have had "success-oriented" mothers . . . who have attempted to raise "success-oriented" children . . . to compete in a "success-oriented" world.

What is success? It has different meanings for everyone. It could include wealth, work status, social acceptance, love, beauty, fame, artistic accomplishment, higher education, etc. Success is sometimes considered to be making choices among these possibilities, deciding what has meaning for you, and finding the best methods for getting what you want.

For me, whatever your formula of success may be, it is important to include feelings of self-love, self-worth, dignity and personal integrity.

As my patients progress in therapy, many of them

become aware that success is equated with fear. They realize they have been unconsciously avoiding success most of their lives. They slowly come to understand the terror success holds for them, and the various ruses and schemes they use to evade it. Before therapy, frightening early childhood experiences block out their memory and their ability to look at this problem. They think they want success "more than anything else in the world."

This idea of avoiding success is unbelievable to most of us. As children we are trained and "geared" for success, so that we can function effectively in our very competitive society.

Therefore, the concept of avoiding success seems absurd. I think if you were to suggest this idea to most people, you'd probably receive this kind of reaction, "Avoid success? Are you crazy? Me! Where is it? I need it. I cherish success. I know how to handle it. I can't get enough of it."

As a therapist, I find this to be one of the basic conflicts——wanting "desperately" to be successful and being "desperately" afraid (unconsciously) to be successful.

RICHARD AND JOYCE

Joyce looks very much like a young hippie with long, black, kinky hair hanging over her shoulders. She washes her hair every day and enjoys drying it in the sun. She says, "I won't be bothered with curlers or any of that fake pretense. I want to be natural and comfortable. I don't care if my hair looks messy. I like it."

Joyce wears very full, long skirts which cover her shoes and long-sleeved peasant blouses with pull-over shawls. Although I have seen her in group therapy for a year, it would be impossible for me to tell you if her breasts were full or small, her legs thin or fat or even whether her rear is firm or fatty. Her figure, under all those clothes, is still a mystery. As a matter of fact, I'm not sure how she gets into the room. She seems to sneak in and out. She is almost ethereal.

On the other hand, her husband Richard is quite a contrast to his wife of ten years. His hair is so perfect it looks like he visits a stylist daily. His wardrobe consists of meticulously tailored Italian suits for work and suede jackets with tight jeans for parties. He has the young, golden boy look . . . he's 6′3″ tall and well built. His clothes fit so perfectly that the details of his body are always very obvious.

Joyce is a professional writer of children's books. She resists her publishers' attempts to get her more involved in work. She prefers to only "dabble a bit."

Richard has been doing very well lately, gaining national prominence with his company. He is being moved up into the management force with a $5,000 annual increase in salary. Instead of being elated by his promotion, Joyce was depressed. She came to talk to me about a recurring nightmare which had been disturbing her.

In the dream, Joyce, her son and Richard were running at night. They were frightened and fleeing from a well-dressed man who was trying to kill her. She ran for help and met a well-dressed woman who wouldn't listen to her. A tidal wave started to overtake them. They reached a safe plateau. But when she turned around, Richard was gone.

Joyce cried as she related her dream. She began to talk about her childhood. "I didn't want to move to a strange neighborhood," she said. "I was afraid to go to a new school. I even asked my parents to stay in our old house because I loved the old neighborhood and all my friends. No matter how much I cried, they wouldn't listen to me. All they cared about was money—houses—success. They didn't care about *me*. Moving away killed my life.

"What was even worse, after my father made more money so we could move to the rich neighborhood, that was the end of him. He travelled so much, I rarely got to see him. So I lost everything—my friends, my school and also my father.

"I've hated money and all that phony hypocrisy ever since. It ruined my life."

In analyzing her recurring nightmare, it became apparent that Joyce replayed what had happened to her when she was ten years old. She carried into the nightmares how frightened she felt in the new neighborhood: how her successful, well-dressed parents *killed* her life and happiness with her old school friends; how neither her mother nor the woman in the dream would listen to her when she pleaded for help; how her father's new wealth, which should have represented a safe plateau, resulted in great losses for her of close childhood friends. . . . And, in this horrible nightmare, Richard was gone. This loss of her husband in the dream also meant a loss of herself. She was lost in the new neighborhood. She was lonely and frightened just as she was on the plateau in the nightmare. In her child's-mind, success had become associated with loss:

Success = loss = loneliness.

When Richard told her about the great successes he was experiencing at work, she was afraid it meant he was going to leave her. And so to counteract and water-down his high feelings, she deluged him with her own success story—how prolific she was and how everyone said she was such a great writer. Or she'd correct his "disgusting" manners and criticize the way he dealt with their son. One night, when he became very excited about a new project while talking to a client on the phone, she accused him of being drunk. She did anything to move him away from the aura or the reality of his success. *She had to stop successful Richard.*

Richard wasn't sure why he felt so down after coming home from work. He usually had the underlying feeling that he had done something wrong.

Richard said to the group one night, "I was almost afraid to have anything good happen to me because I would either be topped by Joyce's accomplishments or criticized when I got home."

What Richard wasn't aware of was that he applied the same sort of put-down to Joyce. They took turns with each other. For openers, Richard actively rebuffed any attempt Joyce made to exploit her beauty. If she put on a bit of rouge or lipstick, he might say, "Gee, honey, I hate to see you put all that junk on your gorgeous skin." If her blouse fit snugly enough to emphasize the shape of her breasts, it was, "You don't have to prove anything, honey. It's much more exciting to have everyone guessing." So, back she went to her long sack dresses.

Richard sabotages Joyce's career as well. Seven years ago her publisher wanted her to tour several major cities and publicize the book she had finished in order to encourage sales. Richard was adamant. "Of course not, no publicity! You're not some phony, publicity-seeking fake. You're a good writer. People will find out about you because of your ability. This isn't a circus side-show. You have talent." The book sold very few copies, even though it was well written. The publisher had predicted this would happen without a structured publicity program. After this event, the publisher avoided handling any major projects with Joyce and lost interest in her work.

What was happening in this case occurs in many relationships. One partner views the success of the other as some sort of loss or withdrawal of their loved one. He or she unconsciously sabotages the success of the other. Both partners usually are active in this kind of play.

I've seen this in relationships where one partner loses a great deal of weight, perhaps as much as fifty pounds. If a wife is fat, a husband may torment or tease her.

But as soon as she begins to lose weight, the husband becomes terrified. "What if she turns into this curvaceous, voluptuous beauty? Maybe she'll even fall in love with someone else and leave me." When they are dieting, many women report to me that their husbands will try to entice them with rich foods and expensive restaurants. In this manner, they subconsciously try to reverse the wife's progress.

In the example above the roles are reversible. The husband could be the fat partner and the wife the enticer-saboteur.

As I discussed earlier, I believe couples find their psychologically similar partners. They seek out the mate who matches their own problems, precisely. Neither Joyce nor Richard was able to handle success, so they each unconsciously chose the other.

Joyce and Richard are gaining insight in their therapy. They are working on their individual problems. Last week Joyce wore a low-necked, knit top and a big smile when she came into her weekly group therapy meeting. It was fun to watch Joyce showing off her femininity for the first time.

MARION AND BOB

Marion, the mother of three daughters, is returning to school at the age of thirty-nine, to get her Ph.D. in history. For years she had been moaning that her husband, Bob, wouldn't let her leave the house, even for a minute. "He wanted to keep me 'barefooted and pregnant;' he didn't want me to be liberated."

Now that Marion is attending school, Bob complains that she either comes home too late, or doesn't give him enough time, and frequently neglects the children. Marion feels that Bob is trying to undermine her success. "He can't stand an intelligent woman," she says.

For the past few months, Marion has been bringing home an extremely bright, male classmate named Steve.

He is twenty-four, tall and very handsome, rugged and athletic looking. Marion and Steve spend many afternoons studying together.

When Bob comes home, Marion often asks, "Oh honey, Steve and I have been studying so long. We're both exhausted. Would you mind if Steve stays for dinner?"

Bob, who is trying to be helpful with Marion's new school career replies, "No, love, I don't mind." Actually, he is so jealous and enraged, that he would like to strangle Steve.

After Steve leaves, Bob starts to verbally "punch" Marion. He says, "Gee, all the kids have colds. The house is a mess. I hate your attending classes. The children haven't been well all this semester, etc."

What Marion and I are working on in her private sessions is the assumption that she is terrified of success. So she challenges Bob to curtail her schooling by scaring him and having her young Lochinvar, Steve, around so much of the time. She shoves Steve into Bob's face almost daily, either by talking about him, or having Steve in the house when Bob comes home. By frightening her husband and making him feel jealous, Marion becomes her own major saboteur.

Bob acted out his part in the sabotage of Marion's school career by NOT telling Marion that he was afraid her school work would pull her away from him. Steve being in their home so frequently reinforced all his fantasies:

School = loneliness = no wife for me.

All Marion understood from Bob was that her time spent on school work prevented her from being an adequate wife and mother. What pulled her away from her husband was his criticism of her mothering and housekeeping skills, not her school work. She didn't understand why he was so critical. She was trying so hard to do a good job as a mother and homemaker, yet, Bob always found something to complain about.

They both came to me to discuss the problem. Bob was finally able to share his fears about Steve.

Marion was honestly surprised. She explained that Steve meant nothing to her; she never thought of him sexually. She had difficulty concentrating on the homework material; being with another student like Steve, really helped. They studied well together.

I asked Marion to put herself in Bob's place. How would *she* feel if every night Bob brought home a great looking secretary and he said, "Honey, I just want to do some dictation. Miss Jones is so efficient, and just because she wears a 38D bra, I don't want you to think I'm a bit interested in her." Marion was better able to understand how Bob felt when the jealousy threat was reversed.

The core of the problem was Marion's fear of success. "I could have been a great historian 'if only' I didn't have the children; 'if only' I weren't a woman; 'if only' I were born twenty years later; 'if only'—etc." Nonsense! It was *she* who almost managed to get her husband to stop the school career by provoking him with her jealous gambit.

Marion couldn't handle success. Although she had finally gotten enough confidence to get out of the house and into school, she was nevertheless forcing her husband to sabotage her.

Most frequently it is my female patients who unconsciously fear and avoid success. This is partly due to the sociological conditioning in our culture. As children, women learn that it is not feminine to be aggressive, competitive or intellectual. Female ambitions are typically channeled towards homemaking and mothering.(1) Women are not encouraged to attend graduate school. So the idea of "no success outside the home," is well established in a young girl's thinking, years before she finds her mate.

(1) Coleman, James C., *Abnormal Psychology and Modern Life.*, Second Edition), Scott, Foresman and Co., Chicago, 1956, p. 356, 357.

Both sexes in the United States maintain the philosophy that if a woman becomes successful, she'll stop being interested in her home and husband. While women do enter colleges in large numbers, recent research has demonstrated that few of them actually graduate.(1) There is too much negative pressure from their husbands, society and more important, from their own early conditioning.

My experience with patients has shown that it is the more independent and successful woman who is most comfortable with herself in marriage. Because she is fulfilled in many areas of her life she has the emotional time to realize how dependent she is on her husband and how much she needs his love. Because she is satisfied and happy with herself during the day, she can be more sharing and giving in the love relationship.

When a woman stays at home, without involving herself in any outside activity of her own, she may feel that her life is dull, empty and without meaning. Her feelings of worthlessness may drive her into some compensating defensive behavior such as extra-marital episodes. She feels so insecure, that she searches for some kind of outside validation in order to fill her up and make her feel complete. Because she feels so unworthy and uninteresting, she is overly occupied with self-examination and self-incrimination. She's just too busy with her SELF to be able to give love to her partner. She's too invested and overwhelmed with her own feelings of nothingness. Her emotional time has been dissipated in recounting her own problems. She has little time left to be loving and giving to her husband.

We are caught in this irony; the route to self-enhancement and self-realization, which includes some kind of meaningful involvement or school experience for the wife, is sabotaged by both partners. Personal success for the woman outside the home, which would

(1) Horner, Matina S., *Femininity & Successful Achievement, A Basic Inconsistency*. In Garskoff, Michele H. (Ed.) *Roles Women Play: Readings Toward Women's Liberation*. Belmont Press, p. 97-122.

ultimately result in her being a happier and more loving wife, is not tolerated because of early childhood conditioning.

PATRICIA

"I know I'm a failure," Patricia lamented during her first meeting with me. "I never seem to be able to finish anything. If I do, it's a mess. Sometimes I think a six-year old is more capable than I am. I feel like an idiot."

Patricia, who is divorced, lives with her teen-aged son and her two cats. Her job as a free-lance photographer brings her in contact with a variety of interesting people. She dates actively but spends the main part of her leisure time at home alone.

As Patricia continued to become more involved in her therapy, I began to detect an emerging pattern. When her work would begin to show signs of leading to more important, better paying assignments, she would suddenly become ill and stay in bed for several days. She would miss deadlines and lose new commissions and was never able to achieve the success level that her talent promised.

Similarly, she'd become ill when she felt more confident about a casual dating relationship showing signs of becoming more permanent.

Patricia and I had been dealing with her pattern of converting impending success into potential failure for several weeks.

Before therapy, she used to consider herself "average . . . mediocre . . . just a run-of-the-mill kind of lady." I was convinced this wasn't true and that Patricia was exceptionally bright. I encouraged her to have some professional evalutions made with a colleague of mine who was researching the area of intelligence testing. When the results came back, I showed them to Patricia. She had scored in the upper 92nd percentile. "I can't believe I'm that smart," she said. "These can't be *my* scores."

As our work continued, Patricia began to accept the new information about herself—she had always been exceptionally intelligent.

Then, why the denial? Why this push towards mediocrity? Why the repetitive cry, "I'm average, I'm mediocre."

Patricia has a great aptitude for commercial photography, but works at it irregularly. She'll work erratically for several months and earn a good deal of money. Then suddenly, she cancels appointments. She'll get into bed feeling like she has the flu, complaining of aches and pains. She'll say something like, "I feel lousy and want to be in bed for awhile. I just can't put my finger on what's wrong. Maybe it's just fatigue. I'm probably just mentally exhausted."

In our work together she confessed, "I know I'm never really sick. When things are going too well, something frightens me and makes me feel anxious. I hate feeling mediocre; yet I actually feel more comfortable when things are just so-so."

When Patricia was very young, her father died. Her mother went into business and became very successful. "As the business expanded, the money poured in," Patricia explained. "My mother was at that store at least twelve hours every day. I hardly ever saw her. There was nothing mediocre about that lady; she was a dynamo."

Patricia told me, "As soon as the relatives heard about my mother's money, they arrived. The leeches moved in. It seemed as though they stayed forever! Maybe I'm afraid to become successful because I don't want leeches hanging around me. You know, doctor, this is the first time I've ever used these words. I've never really thought about this since I was a child. I didn't know I felt like this."

While she was sharing this story with me, I began to see why Patricia was so comfortable with mediocrity, and why she worked so hard at avoiding success. She had put it together in her two-year-old head:

Success = loss of mother = "leeches."

Patricia reported feeling very lonely during the years her mother was in business. Finally her mother remarried, closed the business and returned to being a housewife again. This changed Pat's equation. It now became the following:

Business success terminates = mother back = good life again.

After she recounted this story, Patricia burst into tears. "I want to be cared for," she sobbed. "I want the people I love to be with me. But I don't want any leeches around." Her crying continued. After a while she looked up and said, "Doctor, is this why I always get sick when success seems to be coming my way? Am I afraid of those leeches moving in after all these years? Sounds ridiculous! I don't even have any relatives who would sponge off of me!"

"I'm glad you were able to unblock all those painful feelings," I said. "This will offer you alternative choices. Perhaps when you look at success with your adult eyes, it won't be so frightening for you."

All of us rely on opinions and assumptions that took shape in our minds when we were small children. We continue to refer back to these childhood equations and summations of reality in making our crucial judgments as adults. The problem for Patricia in relying on the data of childhood alone, is that it led her to incomplete and incorrect conclusions that success is associated with unhappiness. This concept is at the base of her present goal of mediocrity. At an early age, Patricia decided that her mother's success was responsible for her unhappy childhood. She has carried this notion with her for over thirty years.

Because Patricia is a highly motivated patient, change is possible despite her early negative associations. Patricia is receptive now to new data about successful people who do lead happy lives and do have loving friends around them.

After a few months of therapy, Patricia started demonstrating significant changes in both her work and social patterns. Her vague illnesses seemed to disappear. She became more enthusiastic about her photography work, her relationships and about herself. Patricia now has a new equation:

From:
Success = no mother = leeches = loneliness.

To:
Success = fun with friends = work you love = feeling good about yourself.

Patricia's homework included repeating the last part of the above formula over and over: Success equals fun, work and good feelings about yourself. She has her new words written on pieces of paper scotch-taped to her bathroom mirror at home, in her date book, on her car seat and desk so she can read them constantly.

Patricia said, "Wherever I look, I see my new formula. Do you suppose it will ever sink into this dumb head of mine?"

"Remember what the tests revealed?" I smiled. "That 'dumb' head of yours is one of the best around."

By permitting new standards and behaviors to enter her adult thinking, Patricia was able to accept healthier and more realistic alternative routes to travel.

Many of us unconsciously destroy our success and operate on rules and formulas put together with our two-year-old heads. These formulas may be totally incorrect, outdated and inappropriate, but we cling to them, reverently. We don't even know they exist, tucked away in our minds like puppet masters, pulling strings that cause us to behave in irrational ways that destroy success.

We can change! Getting a better understanding of our working equations and how we put them together a long time ago is a beginning. When we dare to understand how illogical some of our childhood formulas are, they begin to lose their power to control our lives. We regain our freedom when we develop new adult formulas that consciously include positive feelings about achieving success.

Chapter XV

The Frigid Couple

The frigid female is a myth!

In my work with patients, I have discovered that the frigid female concept frequently disappears when the sexual problems of both partners are examined and understood. I have discovered that such a myth has no foundation. When the psychological aspects of the couple's behaviors are explored, what emerges is the FRIGID COUPLE, not the frigid female.

I find the core of the problem for the frigid couple isn't even sex! The difficulty lies in their INABILITY TO GET CLOSE.

The commonly accepted image of the American male is that he is Mr. Ever-Ready, Mr. Super-Stud and Mr. I Can't Get Enough. Typically, the female assumes the frigid role. "I'm not very interested," she says. "I don't enjoy it. I just do it to please him. I can't wait to get it over with."

The American male deludes himself when he automatically assumes that he is not frigid, and that the sexual problems in his marriage belong to his wife.

It is no accident that the big, wonderful he-man marries the "Not now—I'm too tired" woman. Why would he select her? After all, when he was single, surely he met sexually aggressive females . . . the so-called "I'm ready—let's go" woman. They were available. Why didn't he marry one of those sex-symbols? Why? Because he couldn't handle them emotionally . . . the relationship wouldn't work. They frightened him, or he would have moved towards one of them and become involved in some kind of relationship. He was willing to make a permanent commitment to his "frigid" wife, why not to one of those more "highly sexed" women? He unconsciously understood his fears and avoided the seductive women, except for an infrequent, short-term encounter. He felt anxious and uncomfortable . . . unsure of himself, with the "sexier" women. That is why he chose a wife who clearly evidenced before their marriage, her limited sexual appetite and non-aggressive behaviors. With his wife acting as his "front" and refusing sex most of the time, he could complain loudly and often, "It's all her problem." He could deny the reality of his own frigidity.

Here is a case history that will help you to understand the concept of how the female can accept the total responsibility for all the sex problems in a marriage.

SHIRLEY AND VANCE

Vance owns a sporting goods store in a new shopping center. He can rattle off records set by every champion athlete.

He plays par golf, excellent tennis . . . he's a Mr. Oom-pa-pa of the sports world.

Shirley, our Mrs. Blah, plays the role of the frigid

woman, "I don't want to be bothered with sex. My back hurts tonight. My vagina is sore."

Vance is always ready for intercourse. He wants sex every night—he never gets enough; Shirley never seems to be interested in sex . . . she's too tired. When Shirley and Vance finally do get together, he maintains an erection for hours. During most of that time, Shirley is miserable and uncomfortable. She wants him to have his orgasm. She wants to stop the "Marathon" and get it over with. But Vance insists on continuing . . . it seems like forever for Shirley. She is worried and feels very inadequate about her sexual appetite when she compares herself with Vance.

Shirley is afraid she's frigid, and Vance confirms this continually. She's certain a complete woman—a normal and sensual woman, would enjoy and adore making love to her husband for hours.

Shirley was so concerned about herself sexually that she decided to share this confidential problem with her two closest friends. To her relief, both women agreed they wouldn't want such frequent sex either. One of them exclaimed, "I'd die if my husband wanted to make love for hours every night. I'd be a basket case!"

The problem here wasn't Shirley's frigidity. Her complaints were valid. Genitals *do* become sore after hours of continued sex, and it would be understandable for her to lose interest in love-making under these conditions.

With the new feelings of confidence Shirley gained from sharing with her friends, she was able to come home and talk to Vance more honestly about what was troubling her in their sex life. After much discussion about the problem, and Shirley's insistence, they made the decision to enter therapy.

What we were able to uncover in the weeks of therapy which followed was that Vance had serious sexual problems. He had difficulty having an orgasm with Shirley, because his early childhood sexual formulas didn't include "clean" sex.

He prolonged orgasm, or didn't have one, because he was too frightened to have sexual pleasure under "good," "clean" and "normal" conditions with his wife.

Vance's early sexual education suggested that boys definitely don't have sex with "nice" girls. Vance's understanding of sexual practice indicated that only "whores and dogs" do it. This dogma had been so deeply imbedded in his behavioral framework that he was rarely able to ejaculate unless involved in an oral-genital experience with a prostitute.

Under the protective shroud of the frigid female concept, Vance was able to cover up his sexual difficulties. He remained unaware of his problems by appearing to be an Olympic Sex Champion.

He maintained the aura of Mr. Terrific—Mr. Oom-pa-pa and Shirley remained the sexual failure—Mrs. Blah.

While the Kinsey research([1]) demonstrates that 69% of the total white male population have had some experience with prostitutes, many of these were single experiences. Vance's case was extreme. His sexual satisfaction was restricted to such a narrow range of ejaculation possibilities, usually with a prostitute and only in a particular posture. This was an emotionally crippling and limiting situation for him.

The main tragedy in Vance's hiding behind Shirley's label of frigidity was that he couldn't get help for himself or start working on his own sexual inadequacies and peculiarities.

Essentially, Shirley acted as a front for Vance. He was unable to discuss his own sexual problems, because he felt this threatened his masculinity. Instead, he dignified his problems by selecting a wife who constantly verbalized her disinterest and distaste for sex. As long as one partner picks up the tab for the sexual fears in the marriage, as Shirley did, the other partner remains

(1) Kinsey, Alfred C., Pomeroy, Wardell B., and Martin, Clyde E., *Sexual Behavior in the Human Male*, Philadelphia: Saunders, 1948.

blind. In this case of frigidity, if the female fronts for the responsibility of *their* sex problems, the husband can remain totally unaware of his frigidity or problems.

During the course of therapy, Vance told me he had stopped his involvements with prostitutes; he had finally decided to make a firm commitment to the marriage. It was at this point in therapy that he was able to work on his own sexual problems and get in touch with his *own* frigidity.

When the partners are willing to remain sexually and exclusively in the marital situation, we can look at the actual problems the couple is experiencing. Our repair work of re-examining old, deeply-entrenched value systems and building new, healthy concepts can begin.

If the couple can continue working on the problem of *their* frigidity and their early established fears, an active and satisfying sexual life is possible.

While many of the frigid patients I see are female, it is just as possible for the male to take the frigid role. The sex of the partner is really not important. There is usually one partner who is eager and one partner who is disinterested; these roles are reversible and interchangeable.

Since it takes two people to create and nurture a sexual problem, I will not see a frigid patient alone. I insist on treating both partners who both contribute to the making of the frigid couple.

The unstated and unconscious rule for the frigid couple is that they maintain their sexual distance and don't get too close. There is a terror in sexual intimacy, because it breaks down all distancing barriers. When the so-called frigid woman comes into therapy and is re-educated into new value systems about the normal and healthy aspects of sex, she becomes more relaxed and is willing to participate in more sensual and sexual activities. Then we discover the phenomenon I've witnessed dozens of times with so many couples. As soon as "Mrs. Frigid, Don't Touch-Me-There, Later-

Darling" gets more aggressive and more sexually experimental, a miraculous change takes place in "Mr. Ever-Ready, Let's-Go-To-Bed-Early-Honey." He seems to become sexually unmotivated, sleepy, swamped with work, or in some cases, impotent.

It takes a good deal of hard work in therapy to get the so-called frigid partner to become more active sexually. And throughout this process, "Mr. I Never Get Enough" is reassuring his wife and Doctor Kassorla, "I have no sexual hang-ups. It's my wife's problem. She just doesn't like sex. I love it!" The time comes, if the couple stays in therapy, when the roles become reversed. She wants sex; he's tired.

If the partners are willing to look at the reality that WE are frigid and WE are afraid to get close, change is possible. I am then able to move the couple to a new behavioral plateau where they are *both* interested, involved and sexually motivated.

GOD WASTED GENITALS ON YOU

Maurene plays the role of the "typical frigid woman." She is always pushing away her husband, David, who is constantly hungry for sex. David complains to Maurene, "God wasted genitals on you."

David says he's always feeling rejected, "Maurene is to blame for our sex problems. She thinks only of herself. She doesn't care about me." David is frustrated and confused because they have sex so irregularly. He has been considering divorce during the entire twenty years they've been married.

When I asked him why he never got the divorce, he said, "Well, she has so many nice qualities." What we have found in working together in their therapy is that David's early childhood package included a mother who was very overworked, overwhelmed, and dissatisfied most of the time. Her husband had left when David was only two. David's recall of his mother is that she was always complaining. She had very little money and was swamped with the burden of raising David and his five brothers and sisters. As a result, David was neglected, and received little or no attention or affection. He was a sad child.

Maurene had a similar childhood background. She was given little affection. Her father was an alcoholic who frequently beat both Maurene and her mother. She was terrified to be near her father even when he was in a good mood. She never knew when he might "turn on her."

Whatever affection Maurene was able to give him, David was never satisfied. He nagged her constantly, and it seemed as if she always had a hungry animal on top of her. This image has become so vivid to Maurene, she doesn't even want to start any lovemaking, because she knows she will feel like a failure when they are finished. David will inevitably say, "Boy, that was great. . . . I can't wait until we do it again. . . . I wish we could do this all night."

Maurene thinks, "There's something wrong with me—I can't seem to please him. The minute we're finished he's talking about next time. I feel like he's a bottomless well. I'm exhausted. Surely, if I were a really sexy woman he'd feel satisfied at least for a while."

Maurene reports that she so dreads David's animal insatiability that she abhors the whole idea of sex; when he touches her, she is repelled.

To compound the problem, Maurene had a very unfortunate early sexual education in which she learned to associate sex with being "used." Her mother would say to her, "Watch out for men. They want to 'use' you for a receptacle." As a result, Maurene feels she's being taken advantage of and she doesn't consider sex pleasurable.

In Maurene's mind, David was always using her. "He hugs me only when he wants sex," Maurene complains. "David doesn't want the real me. He just wants to 'use me' as a sex object. Otherwise he never comes near me."

I have developed exercises that I give to couples, to help them learn to tolerate more affection and get closer to one another. With Maurene and David, I suggested they hug each other every night for a week. The only rule I emphasized was that the hugging be nonsexual, that is, not be a prelude to sexual intercourse. Rather, they were to hug and kiss and then go to sleep in each other's arms.

This 'no sex' rule is very important. The premise I keep restating is that the problem for frigid couples is not sex, it is getting close. My hugging exercise helps them to get close without having the anxiety of dealing with their sexual fears.

I explained this exercise to Maurene and David. Maurene said she was willing and happy to participate.

The rule was stated clearly in my office; no sex during this exercise. Both partners agreed. On the first night of the exercise, Maurene was smiling and eager to hug David. After about two minutes, David said that he wanted to have intercourse. Maurene felt as though she had been hit with a bat. She was completely turned off, "David, why can't you keep your word? You promised to just hug me. I wanted to hug. I hate you for stopping it!" She pushed him away and didn't want to continue the exercise. My hunch is David became anxious. The experience of hugging without sex was too uncomfortable for him. He had no skills for just enjoying the fun and closeness of hugging.

He stopped the *strange* behavior—affection.

He started the *familiar* behavior—intercourse.

Maurene was in the same place in terms of childhood experience. She hadn't learned how to be affectionate as a little girl, either. She probably would have stopped the hugging if David hadn't done so first.

David's training as a child was in complaining and feeling neglected. When Maurene's arms were around him, he reported feeling uneasy. He knew how to get her to push him away——he started talking about sex.

Maurene felt he had "turned on her" in the hugging exercise. "It's all *his* fault," she said.

"Maurene," I interrupted, "my hunch is you were just as uneasy and anxious about getting close as David was."

"That's true," Maurene admitted. "I felt relieved when David tried to make love. I had an opportunity to complain and stop the exercise. The hugging without sex did scare me."

"Good," I said. "That's very perceptive, Maurene. I'm glad you're willing to take a look and SEE.

"Neither of you is responsible for what you missed during your childhood. For both of you to change, it's necessary to look into your family backgrounds where the genesis of your present problem rests. You *are* on more familiar territory when complaining and creating distance. You have little experience with hugging and affection."

"I haven't any sex problems," David said indignantly. "Maurene just admitted to you, Doctor, that it was she who wanted to stop the exercise. That proves it's *her* problem."

"David," I said. "You prohibit change when you focus on 'Maurene's problems.' You need to realize that you are frigid also; you both are. That's why you selected each other and have stayed together for twenty years, complaining all the time.

"In your sex patterns, only one of you can want sex at a time, while the other needs to move back.

"David, I believe you push sex on Maurene, as you unconsciously know it will force her away. You need a good deal of distance between you. This is the way you remember it with your mother. If I tried to push food into your mouth, you'd never want it, even if you were hungry." I walked up to David and tried to force the cup of coffee I was holding into his mouth. He turned his head away, looking annoyed, and put his hands up to stop me. "See how you tried to stop me?" I said. "What I've just done to you is very distasteful and unpleasant. It was appropriate for you to push me away. This is how Maurene feels about your sexual behavior with her, so she pushes you away."

"There's right, David," Maurene added. "I do love you and want to get closer. But I always have to be on my guard with you and make sure you won't force yourself on me the way the Doctor forced her coffee on you. I'll bet you didn't like it, David. Neither do I!"

David said thoughtfully, nodding his head, "I see what you mean . . . I didn't know it felt so awful. I think I understand, honey. I did feel I had to guard myself when that coffee was pushed in my face. I wouldn't have taken even a sip—no matter what. It was awful to feel pushed like that. I hated it.

"I really know what you're saying. Maybe I do push sex so Maureen will say no. I never dreamed that it was *me* who was stopping the sex. I can't believe it. But maybe you're right. Maybe I am afraid. According to you, Doctor, I guess this makes me frigid, too!"

"That's good work, David," I said. "You're starting to put it together. I believe we'll be able to work on change now. You both sound ready to take a look at your problems and stop the blaming. GOOD!"

MOVING AWAY FROM FRIGIDITY

Eileen and Tom are in their early thirties. He's building up his practice as a dentist, and Eileen is his nurse. They enjoy working together. They have no children.

Sex has always been a problem in their twelve-year old marriage. Eileen could go for months without intercourse, yet she reports being very much in love with her husband.

Tom said he was seeing another woman. He explained he was a normal, sexual man and since his wife was frigid, he needed to go outside of the marriage for sex. It was after confessing this to Eileen that they decided to come to me for help.

When he finally admitted he was involved in an affair with another woman, Eileen was relieved. She felt happy he was having sex with someone else and not bothering her. She loved him and wanted the marriage, but she didn't want any sex. After a while, they both became worried about the survival of their marriage, which is why they came in for therapy.

Tom reported that he enjoyed wonderful sex with the other woman. She couldn't get enough of him. With Eileen, sex was awful. She acted as though she couldn't stand his body and wanted nothing to do with him sexually.

Tom felt Eileen hated sex, and was just performing out of a sense of duty. When he had an orgasm, she found it abhorrent and immediately took a shower. If he ever ejaculated on her body, she acted as though acid had been spilled on her and jumped out of bed like Lady Macbeth to wash out the "foul spot." He felt despised and neglected.

We worked together for several weeks on the premise that they were both frightened of sex, and that it wasn't just Eileen's problem. This idea was impossible for Tom to grasp for a long time. Finally, he became more involved in our work and started discussing *his* sexual fears, hurts and problems. Soon after, Tom reported, "I'm not sure why, but I've lost interest in my girlfriend. I'm not going to see her anymore." At this juncture they were able to zero in on *their* problems.

They worked on their anger and disappointments in sex. Tom explained, "It makes me feel awful that you don't think I'm attractive or desirable when we're having sex. I know you don't enjoy my body. That really hurts me. I feel I'm repulsive to you whenever you don't caress me."

"It's not your body," Eileen said. "It's because you're always insisting we have sex. I'm afraid to undress when you're around. I'm afraid to even touch you because I'm certain you'll think I want to have intercourse. You don't think of anything else!"

"Hell! You haven't wanted intercourse since our dating days," Tom broke in. "Even then, you were hurting my feelings and criticising me. I felt rotten when you said I was a lousy lover."

"I'm really surprised," Eileen answered. "I had no idea I had hurt your feelings. I never dreamed anything I said would make a significant impression on you. I always thought you felt you were perfect. I didn't know you were sensitive or ever took my remarks seriously. I didn't even know it was hard for you to talk about feelings until we got into therapy. I was certain you were totally confident. I thought you never felt inadequate."

"I was afraid to talk like this to you. I thought you'd find me even more repulsive if I sounded hurt or told you how worried I really am," Tom said.

"Oh, Tom! I'm glad to hear you're human! It makes me feel closer to you." Eileen went on, "I thought I was the *only* one who felt inadequate sexually. I always felt there was something wrong with me. And I hated you for your perfection! I thought I had some important feminine part missing because I'm rarely interested in sex."

"That's another thing that hurts me," Tom said. "You seem to be doing me a favor on the few occasions when we do have sex. I hate that! There are other women who think I'm *great* in bed."

"Tom, that was a low blow," I said. "My hunch is, you're still feeling deeply wounded that Eileen called you a lousy lover. You haven't expressed all your feelings yet. Are you afraid Eileen will find you repulsive if you do? She didn't a minute ago when you told her how you felt. She came closer to you. What else is there, Tom? What's left that hurts?"

Tom started crying, "I've been too afraid to even think about this. I've been busy cheating and bragging about what a great man I am in bed. This has been a cover up for my insecurities. Actually, I feel like a failure in bed, because Eileen can't stand me sexually and has always pushed me away. I feel so bad. I don't know what to do."

As he continued crying, Eileen moved over next to him and put her arm around him. "Honey, you're wonderful in bed—perfect! You're way off. That's not why I don't want to have sex. It's because having sex is *always your idea.* I've felt I had to be accommodating. You make all the decisions. I have no choice. I'm like a child with you. *I want choice*!"

"He doesn't have a machine gun, Eileen," I said. "You do have choice. You're an adult. No one can *make* you feel or act like a child. No one can make you have sex. He doesn't rape you! You can say 'yes' or 'no' when he asks. You have a mouth, USE IT!"

"That's fine with me, honey," Tom agreed. "I *want* you to have a choice. It's no fun for me if you're doing me a favor. I like your emphasis on 'only when I feel like it.' That's great for me, too. It makes me feel safer. Then I'll know you really want to be with me. I'd love that."

Only a few days after Eileen's declaration about wanting choice, an amazing change took place. Eileen was becoming very involved sexually with Tom and seemed to enjoy it. When she no longer felt guilty about refusing to have sex, her desire to make love increased.

It also has been a liberating, eye-opening experience for Tom. He was too frightened to get in touch with his feelings, so he blocked them out. Until our work together, he was unable to experience his fear of being inadequate. He defended against the fear with his extra-marital behavior and by bragging about his superior sexual performance with other women.

Tom had been certain their sexual problems were Eileen's fault, and that she just wasn't the sexy type. He never had a chance to examine his own frigidity, because Eileen was accepting the blame for their sex problems at home, or Tom was busy having sex outside of the marriage.

The focus for both of them now is on improving their sex life. Tom is willing to talk and laugh about his problems. He reported recently that one night when he and Eileen were both feeling loving and happy, she grabbed his hand and led him to the couch. Giggling, she dimmed the lights and unbuttoned her blouse.

Suddenly, he became anxious and blurted out, "Oh honey! I don't have any time. I have to take out the trash!"

He came into his next session smiling. He realized what had happened and he was laughing and shaking his head about it. He said, "You won't believe this, Kassorla. I must be crazy! My wife threw her breasts in my face the other night, and I wanted to wrestle with trash barrels. I knew at the time I sounded peculiar, but all I wanted to do was get out! Can you believe it? The trash is the last thing in the world that is important to me. How frigid can you get? Trash barrels instead of sex! Hey, Doc! Maybe I'm going bananas!"

"You sound fine to me, Tom," I said. "You're being very undefensive; you're willing to SEE what's happening in your sex life. That's good work."

Once Tom was able to admit his own frigidity and Eileen was able to have choice with her love-making, their sexual life gradually changed and improved. Now, they take turns initiating sex. Eileen says she feels much more affectionate, "We hug much more and I'm really experiencing more pleasure and loving feelings for Tom."

"Me, too!" Tom was smiling. "Doctor, I think you ought to know that my interest in having intercourse with other women has absolutely melted away. If Eileen says no to sex and just wants to hug, I am perfectly content. Also, I thought you'd be pleased to know that my interest in trash barrels seems to have melted away. I must be cured!"

Chapter XVI

I Want Sex

The two most difficult words for new patients to say while they are having sex is "I WANT." When they want something sexually, they are like the psychotic child we talked about earlier. They use indirect methods which are almost as damaging as hitting their heads against the wall. They prefer to be devious, use gambits, conceal, hide, lie,—anything but say, "I WANT." It is as though they become mute in bed. This results, in part, in the sexual dysfunction and problems that can be found in over 50% of the married couples in this country.(1)

We learn to hide what we want and lie about sex by modeling from our parents' behavior. I doubt if many among you have heard your grandmothers or mothers brag about their pre-marital sex. Most of my

(1) Runciman, Alex P., *Sex and Aging,* Paper presented to the American Medical Association National Meeting, Miami, Florida, 1968.

new patients would be very surprised if they discovered that mother wasn't a virgin before her wedding. Yet, research demonstrates it is unlikely that mother or grandmother were virgins when they got married.(1)

When I attended a conference in Greece,(2) about the "Changing New Family," the only behavior mentioned that *hadn't* changed in this century were sexual practices. There *has been* a change in openness and talking—little or no change in actual behavior. One scientist reported that there has been only a 7% increase in pre-marital sex in the last thirty years! "Seven percent!" another scientist laughed and added, "That's actually nothing. I'll bet the price of eggs, butter, and rent have gone up 300 percent in the last thirty years!"

When you hear people talking about the moral decay of the new generation in relation to sex, remember this 7% figure. The only real change is that young people don't hide and lie as previous generations did about how they felt and what they wanted sexually.

Most of the couples I treat have some kind of sexual problem.

A new case I treated recently illustrates how difficult it is to say "I WANT" in a sexual setting.

CATHY & JOHN

Cathy and John are a delightful, vivacious pair. They are fun to be with. Cathy, who is a thirty-three year old housewife, enjoys raising her three-year old daughter Michele. While the child is in nursery school, she attends junior college part-time and is working for a degree in Sociology. John is a teacher who specializes in children with perceptual problems. He is the same age as Cathy. They are very much in love.

Cathy came to see me alone, unhappy because she

(1) Kinsey, Alfred C., Pomeroy, Wardell B., and Martin, Clyde E., *Sexual Behavior in the Human Male,* Philadelphia: Saunders, 1948.
(2) Second International Delphic Colloquium on Family Therapy. Cypress, Greece. May 29, 1972.

was unable to experience orgasms. On her first visit, she cried and said, "I feel inhuman. Why can't I have orgasms? Everyone else does. What's wrong with me, I don't even feel like a woman; I feel so different."

I corrected Cathy, "Everyone else *doesn't* have orgasms, Cathy. This is a very common problem. Orgasms can be available to you. We can work on this in your therapy. The other women I've treated have been able to have an orgasm after doing the exercises I recommended and bringing their husbands in to work on the problem with them."

"Actually, it isn't so important that I have an orgasm. I'm not so sure I care. I can live without them," Cathy said.

I reassured her the problem wasn't a major one, and she'd probably have orgasms before long.

"Orgasm is part of the sexual experience," I said. "Just as I think it is important for you to be able to taste, experience and enjoy all the beautiful foods on a banquet table, I feel it is important for you to be able to taste, enjoy, and experience all the beautiful parts of your sexual self. Orgasm is one of these parts—a very satisfying healthy, normal and good-feeling part.

"I feel you are emotionally crippled when you are unable to open one door of your body. It is as though I say to you, 'Here is a fine house—it is a 'Cathy' house. You can go into every room, but stay away from the door that has the sign 'Orgasm' written on it. Do not touch that door. It is locked. Stay out!'

"It is normal and healthy for you to be able to open up every door of your sexual house—I don't want you to have any locked places."

On her second session, Cathy came into my office looking very upset. "John is furious with me. We've been fighting for two days. He doesn't want me to go shopping at my favorite market anymore. I hate that authoritarian, bossy husband."

I asked Cathy to tell me what happened before they started fighting.

"Everything was all right until he came home the other night. He said I looked 'high' and asked me what happened during the day. I told him I went shopping for groceries and had so much fun. I wore a tight sweater today," I explained to him. "And those silly clerks were all whistling at me. It certainly boosted my morale."

"That's a very frightening message, Cathy. No wonder John was furious. What did you expect?"

"What I expect is for him to get the idea that I have beautiful breasts that other men appreciate. And he better start appreciating them. I want him to kiss my breasts. I realize I've never really asked him to—but he should know. Don't all men know? That turns me on. I love that. I want him to realize I have breasts," she said angrily as she pointed to herself.

"Cathy, neither John, nor any man, will know what you want unless you tell him. There is no information in your story that will enable John to decipher the message, 'I want you to kiss my breasts.' If that's what you want, tell him—straight, *out-of-your-mouth*, not through your market story. That will just paralyze him with fear. And those breasts of yours will never get kissed, he'll be so worried."

"You know, Doctor, the whole market story wasn't even true. I just lied to wake him up a little. I *did* want him to worry. I'm afraid to ask John for anything while we're having sex. He might think I'm cheap. Besides if he said *no* to me, I'd be so humiliated."

"Cathy, lies and schemes will just pull you and John farther apart. I know it's difficult to say what you want directly. We'll work on that. It is important for you to get back to John and tell him you lied. If you explain you were afraid to tell him directly and say 'I WANT,' he'll understand. Also, he'll be relieved and won't worry about the market."

"I guess he would be relieved. Besides, during sex,

he can't say 'I want' either," Cathy said. "He probably will understand why I lied."

"Good," I said. "You're right. You're a matched pair; no 'I wants.' That's why you're married. Neither one of you can talk when it comes to sex."

Before Cathy left the office, we talked about her childhood. Whenever she said, "I want" as a little girl, her mother would make fun of her or call her selfish. She would say, "I'm sick of your, 'I want candy, I want ice-cream, I want cookies.' All I hear from you Cathy is 'I want.' It's selfish to always think of yourself. I'm your mother, a grown woman and I don't get what I want. Settle down and wake up—no one gets what they want in this world. . . . etc."

Often, when parents have difficulty saying "no," they punish their children for saying "I want." In this case, the parent would unconsciously think, "If I can stop that little one from saying 'I want,' then it won't matter that I can't say 'no.' I won't need to say 'no' if only the child stops saying 'I want.' I've got to get him to stop."

Cathy's mother was successful. The "I wants" stopped when Cathy was little.

There are some patients who can say "I want" in non-sexual settings. However, like Cathy, when they are with their partners they become mute or devious when it comes to asking for something sexual for themselves in a direct way.

I've developed an exercise to help patients say, "I want" in a sexual situation. I gave this exercise to Cathy. I explained to her, "This exercise is for you and John to practice together at home. It is a preliminary exercise designed to help couples express their feelings and their needs during sex. I'm also including a 'Hugging Exercise' for you and John to work on.

"This one is just for you, Cathy," I said, handing her some other papers. "It's a masturbation exercise. It will help you become more familiar with, and better able to enjoy your own body."

Cathy and John came in to see me together on the third session. Cathy had told him about her lying. He said, "I didn't realize I was so hard on Cathy that she was afraid to ask me for something when we make love. I feel bad. What's wrong with me that I'm so hard to talk to?"

"John," I said, "you're wasting your time blaming yourself. You haven't been hard on Cathy. That's not the problem. There's nothing wrong with either you or Cathy. Most people have some kind of sexual problem. Your difficulty as a couple is that neither one of you can say 'I WANT.' Few people can communicate their needs to the one they love. You, at least, are willing to look at your problems and do something about them. Now I want to talk about your homework. How did the exercise work go?"

Cathy explained that neither she nor John could get to any of the exercises. "He stalled around every night. He'd be busy working on his model planes, or phoning clients or something."

"Cathy, once we start blaming John we won't be able to make any changes. We'll get bogged down with who's naughty and who did what. And besides, you had a mouth last week. Where were you? Stop the blaming! Rather," I said, "each of you needs to say: 'How did I evade the homework? . . . What did I do? . . . Was I too frightened to proceed? . . . How did I delay?' "

The blaming work took several more sessions. By the second month of therapy, they were able to start the exercises. The blaming had stopped, and each one of them was sharing their fears and their inability to be sensual.

Under hypnosis, in separate sessions, they talked about their earliest sexual experiences. My goal in using hypnosis at this point in their therapy, was to get them to re-experience their childhood feelings and attitudes about sex and help them to re-associate new, healthy adult words with sex. As children, they learned that playing doctor and other sexual games was "dirty and nasty" and had to be concealed and hidden. Through hypnosis, they were able to go back and recapture some of those moments and associate their new words with sex such as, "healthy, normal, fun, pleasure, enjoy and sensual."

By the third month of therapy, Cathy was practicing her masturbation exercise regularly when she was alone during the day. She explained to me, "I think I'd be too frightened to do this without your written instructions, Doctor. The exercises have really helped John and me. Now we're able to work on them together. They're actually fun . . . and I feel so much closer to John."

By the fifth month of therapy, she had reached her first orgasm. Cathy came into her session elated, "I did it! I did it! Imagine! I had an orgasm!"

The following are the exercises that John and Cathy worked on in therapy.

ROBOT or "I WANT" EXERCISE

A robot is a mechanical human-like machine that has no feelings and doesn't think. The robot has a master who gives all the commands or "I WANTS," and the robot carries out his orders. In this exercise, we use the robot-master concept. One partner plays the worker-robot one night while the other partner is the Commander who gives the orders, receives the pleasure and does nothing in return.

This will be reversed on the second night when the other partner becomes the worker. The retiring robot now becomes the Commander who gives the instructions and receives the fun and pleasure.

On the first night, if they like, the couple may start the exercise in the bathtub. Set the scene: lights low, your favorite music playing, no distractions, take the phone off the hook and lock the door. Lovers need a lock on their door to insure privacy. Have a chilled bottle of wine with glasses in the bathroom. Keep some kind of oil or emollient near by that you enjoy having rubbed on your skin. Once you're both in the water, the wife, who is tonight's Commander, gives the sexual orders, "Robot, *I want* you to wash my back with soap . . . gently . . . rub very slowly . . . that feels wonderful . . . *I want* you to play with my feet . . . more slowly dear Robot . . . good . . . keep doing that . . . *I want* you to kiss my neck . . . no biting, Robot . . . slowly . . . gently . . . *I want* you to rub my arms . . . good . . . I *want* some wine now Robot . . . etc."

Once in bed, the Robot exercise continues with the same partners in the same roles. "Robot, *I want* you to rub my body very gently," continues the wife . . ."*I want* you to use just your finger tips . . . that's wonderful . . . Robot, *I want* you to massage my legs now . . . with oil . . . harder . . . good . . . keep doing that . . . press down . . . more . . . fine . . . rub my back again . . . more oil . . . gently . . . I want you to turn me over now robot . . . rub my stomach slowly . . . etc."

What is important in this exercise is that the Master, or Commander and the robot maintain their roles throughout the episode. This exercise stops only when the Master for the evening is satisfied, and has asked for everything he or she wants.

On the second evening, the wife takes the Robot role. The husband, now the Commander, gives the instructions and reverses the procedures of the night before. Again, the "role playing" would be maintained. Only when the Commander is entirely satisfied does the exercise stop, and the Robot-worker is finished.

After a few sessions of playing "Robot," my patients report feeling happier, playful, more content and more loving with each other. I have my patients continue playing Robot until they feel at ease in saying "I want" when having sex. This usually takes several months of practicing the Robot exercise. Then this exercise can be put aside, and perhaps reintroduced at a later time when both partners agree and feel it will be rewarding for them to play Robot again.

It is interesting to note that once the Robot exercise has been introduced, patients find they are saying "I WANT" in other non-sexual situations to their colleagues, parents, employees, friends, etc. They even report their children are using "I wants" with them. For example, John was bragging, "Doctor, I love what's happened to Cathy and me in our love-making, and you should hear my little three-year old Michele. She says, "Daddy, I wantsa this, and Daddy, I wantsa that." She's so cute, she can't even say it right—but she sure knows what she "Wantsa!"

HUGGING EXERCISE

I have another exercise that is designed to shatter some of the old taboos and myths about sex. It will help you and your partner to be more sensual. The entire exercise is broken down into individual sessions; I recommend they be practiced on separate days. It is more rewarding to move at a slow pace rather than to do two exercises in one day.

On the first session, you and your partner are to lie down, unclothed, side-by-side in a quiet, private place without outside noises to divert your thoughts. Each partner is to start exploring his own body, alone, without attending to or being concerned with the other. The objective is to hug, explore, caress and gently touch each part of *you.*

> During each session of the exercise think to yourself, "This is healthy, this is normal, this is good, this is fun. It is fun to enjoy my body."

Start at your face and very slowly and gently run your hands and fingers over your forehead. Close your eyes. Relax. Enjoy. Explore the ins and outs, the hard places, the soft places, where it is round, where the hair meets the skin, the bony spots, the openings. Explore slowly in detail every part; take your time. Slowly proceed to the other parts of your face and the rest of your body. Get acquainted with *you.*

On this first night, avoid the erotic areas. This first step is a non-sexual introduction to your body. The person you love is beside you, sharing and participating in the experience with his own body.

In the second session, the exercise of hugging yourself continues, initially, much the same way: each partner exploring his/her own body, *without* concern for his/her partner, while relaxing and enjoying. Get acquainted with yourself, all the different places and parts —slowly, gently. During this time you will both include the more erotic, sensual areas of your own body. The female will touch and feel her breasts, her buttocks, her thighs, and other erogenous zones and/or whatever other areas stimulate and excite her. Or she may want to exclude one of these areas. The movement as before, is very slow, very gentle. Get acquainted with the ins and outs, the soft places, the harder places, the openings, the hair, the feel of the different surfaces. Enjoy this healthy, good fun.

By himself, the male is also touching and feeling his own erotic areas. Slowly, gently. Relax. Enjoy your body. It's fun, it's healthy.

On the third session, the partners can explore each other non-sexually and essentially re-cycle session one. Only this time, they do it *together*. One partner may slowly and gently touch and explore the other's body, each part, each place. Perhaps, he may touch his or her own body in the same place, then slowly and gently explore other parts of his partner's body . . . in relaxed motions. The movement is back and forth from one body to the other—hugging, caressing, touching, exploring. Erotic areas will be avoided during this third, *together* session. The pace is slow and gentle. Practice only one exercise per day, although it is fine to play more than once each day. Don't move on to exercise 4 on the same day you begin exercise 3. Keep the pace very slow and gentle. Don't rush . . . relax . . . enjoy.

I hope when you're alone you'll hear and say these words over and over again in your head: "slow . . . gentle . . . explore . . . enjoy . . . get-acquainted . . . fun . . . exciting . . . stimulating . . . healthy . . . good . . . sensual . . . slow . . . gentle, etc." Read them again. Repeat them to yourself.

It is important to substitute these new, healthy words about your body and your sensuality for your old non-functional, non-accurate and non-pleasurable words.

Exercise 4 is similar to exercise 2, and includes erotic activities, performed together. The male may first play with and enjoy his wife's body, then fondle his own body. This back and forth movement continues for both partners. It is important to proceed slowly, gently, exploring, hugging, enjoying. Or he may massage his body with one hand while he is playing with his wife using his other hand.

The female will be involved in this same back and forth movement, enjoying her body and her partner's body, sometimes simultaneously, at other times separately—slowly, gently, having fun.

REMEMBER, that during all these sessions you are thinking to yourself: "This is normal, this is healthy, this is good, this is fun. It is healthy to enjoy my own body and my partner's body."

Many patients report that after this hugging exercise, they are able to incorporate the back and forth flow of ME enjoying myself and WE enjoying each other during coitus.

For example, one female patient told me, "I never before felt good about touching my breasts or my vagina. Since our hugging exercise, I often play with my breasts and sometimes I'm able to massage my own body while my husband is making love to me. It's fun. I'm enjoying myself and our sex more. And you know what, Doctor? Since our sex is better, we don't seem to be battling and arguing about the children so much anymore."

EXERCISE FOR THE NON-ORGASMIC FEMALE

I would like to consider the problems of the non-orgasmic female, a condition which is prevalent both in the United States and in Britain. About 40% of my female patients are non-orgasmic at the onset of therapy. I have heard colleagues report as many as 90% of their female patients are non-orgasmic.

Fortunately, I have found the problem to be correctable in most cases. It is not a serious condition to treat, and the prognosis is good. I find that if patients do the exercises, share feelings, and go slowly, they usually do reach orgasm.

I have had considerable success by using methods which focus on masturbation exercises. Masturbation or autoeroticism is producing an orgasm or sexual excitement by manipulation of your own genitalia.

Often, I find my patients come into therapy with negative feelings about masturbation. Some of the feelings are religiously based and some are culturally based. It is important to note that the religious taboos have been considerably modified. As recently as 1967, there was a marked moderation on the view of masturbation among Catholic leaders.([1])

Most often, negative values are transmitted directly to the child by the parents. When I talk about masturbation, I am speaking only as a psychologist, and do not wish to get involved in moral or cultural issues. I want to limit my comments about masturbation to a psychological point of view. In this regard, masturbatory behavior is normal and healthy.

Masturbatory play in the United States is less prevalent than in the European or Eastern countries, where I

(1) McInnes, A.G., *Roundtable on the Moral Aspects of Sex Counseling by Physicians*, Medical Aspects of Human Sexuality, 1 Sept. 1967, p. 61.

have also treated patients. However, research suggests that masturbation is more acceptable among the educated social classes in this country. "Masturbation is clearly a very important outlet for the better educated: It is used by almost all college-educated males and nearly two-thirds of the females."(1)

Many of my patients are frightened to masturbate. As children, their mothers assured them the consequences would involve some kind of physical or psychological damage to their bodies. This is nonsensical folk-lore.

I have found cross-masturbation to be a common occurrence during sex play with many couples. This is certainly normal activity. Each partner brings his mate to orgasm either in mutual concert or with one partner working alone on his or her mate. Either arrangement is fine and can be very satisfying.

In order to counteract the neglect and aversion to self-masturbation that I find so prevalent, especially in my female patients, I have designed exercises to break-down her early negative conditioning. The goal here is to introduce masturbatory skills into her sexual repertoire. These exercises are an important prelude to helping the non-orgasmic female reach orgasm.

MASTURBATION EXERCISE

Session one of this exercise can be borrowed directly from the Hugging Exercise with this exception, I recommend the female patient be *alone* in a private, comfortable setting where she can feel safe and separate.

If you'll remember, Hugging Session #1 involved exploring and enjoying one's body in great detail, avoiding erotic areas and moving very slowly and gently while thinking, "This is fun, normal, healthy, sensual behavior." This is also the first session of *this* exercise.

(1) Katchadourian, Herbert A., and Lunde, Donald T. *Fundamentals of Human Sexuality,* Holt, Rinehart and Winston, Inc., New York, 1972.

Many of my patients report they enjoy using lightly scented body oils during this exercise. Baby oil also works very well. Explore. Enjoy your own body.

Session two (on the second day,) again follows the Hugging Exercise. You will hug and feel all the areas of your body and this includes touching and massaging all your erogenous zones. Focus on all the erotic areas and places of pleasure you enjoy. Your thinking is important. Use your new healthy words: "fun . . . exciting . . . gently . . . explore . . . get acquainted . . . enjoy."

Carefully re-read exercises one and two of the Hugging Exercise to help you remember the specific steps. Move slowly. Relax. Enjoy.

Session three (on third day,) encompasses only the erotic zones. The woman slowly massages and caresses her body, focusing on her breasts, genitals and other areas she find pleasurable. She proceeds at whatever pace feels comfortable for her. Usually patients report their movements slower at the onset and move towards crescendo as their excitation increases. Use and repeat your new healthy words. Enjoy your body. Have fun.

With some of my patients, it takes several months to reach orgasm using these exercises. Still others reach orgasm by the end of the first month of working with their bodies. Once having achieved the first orgasm, they can often experience several orgasms during their exercises. Each woman discovers what works best for her.

Whatever feels good is fine. *There is no right way to masturbate.* Your way is best for you.

Once the female is comfortable with her own body, she can better explain to her partner what excites and stimulates her. She is able to show him the "right" places where it feels good for her. She can teach him how to proceed to help her reach an orgasm.

Approaching orgasm may be very frightening to the woman who has been non-orgasmic. Some patients have explained they fear they are going "crazy" when feeling very excited and approaching orgasm. This fear is common. Don't worry. You will adapt and become less frightened after more practice. Share your fears when you are with your partner. He can then be more loving and supportive. He can help you, perhaps to rest for while. Then, resume the fun, good feelings and pleasure of enjoying your own healthy body.

EDUCATIONAL SEX

I encourage patients to share sexual experiences with their partners via all the available media——books, films, and magazines.

There are many beautiful books you could read with your lover. The better books usually include good art work and are filled with humor. Here are two, some of my patients enjoy.[1] [2]

Don't worry about your children seeing these books. They usually look for awhile and then run off to their other activities. Sociologists have suggested that children and adults are attracted to the "forbidden" in sex. "A society with liberal attitudes towards sexual expression is likely to have less sexual behavior than a culture that places sanctions on such expressions."[3]

There is a recently comprised report on pornography which suggests that adults who have developed normal sexual behavior have had more exposure to pornography during their teen-age years than people who grow up with sexual deviances.[4]

Two years ago, when I was on a world-lecture tour, I spent some time in India. The Temples were of particular interest to me. The exterior walls were covered

(1) Kronhausen, Eberhard and Kronhausen, Phyllis. *Erotic Art,* Grove Press Inc., New York, 1968.
(2) Rawson, Phillip, *Erotic Art of the East,* G.P. Putnams' Sons, New York, 1968.
(3) Winick, C., *The Desexualized Society.* In *The New Eroticism,* (Ed.) P. Noble, New York: Random House, 1970, p. 201-207.
(4) Goldstein, Michael J., Kant, Harold S. and Hartman, John J., *Pornography and Sexual Deviance,* University of California Press, 1973.

with erotic figures copulating. Large numbers of adults, mostly foreign tourists like myself, examined these walls, but not a single Indian child could be seen showing any interest. They'd be off playing near-by. It just wasn't *that* special for them, because erotica is a normal part of their daily environment.

When I was a post-doctoral intern, I treated adult patients who were extreme sexual deviants. Their sex was limited to bizarre behavior such as attacking children, exposing their genitals around school grounds or being able to copulate only with animals, etc. Without exception, they had no sexual education or exposure to pornography as children. One of these patients reported to me that he was brutally beaten by his father for asking what the word "penis" meant. When I worked with a pregnant thirteen-year old in London, she had no sexual information; the same was true for the teen-age boy who had sex regularly with his eight-year old sister.

In an earlier chapter, I noted that sexually promiscuous teen-age girls had little or no sexual education. Sex for them was some mysterious, magical, unknown and "forbidden fruit" that *had* to be explored. Children with accurate, honest sexual information grow up to be very discriminating, responsible and selective. They are the ones who are most likely to wait for an important love relationship.

Reach out for the professionally researched sex data that is available to you. Allow it to become a natural and integral part of your family's total growth picture.

In relation to the discussions and case histories I've presented concerning sexual behavior, my objective has been to add new data to your personal libraries of sexual information. I've wanted to give you many new choices that could help you to expand your sexual functioning. I hope they will offer you a variety of new ways to view yourself and your partner, sexually.

In approaching the area of sex, my goal has been

to present alternatives for your consideration . . . alternate routes for you to travel.

Recently, an excellent and comprehensive collection of research material was gathered and organized, which discusses sex education and morality. In this study they suggest, "Alternatives are values that need not be held in common by the members of a society. A great many of our values dealing with sex—once considered to be universals to which everybody had to pay unquestioned allegiance—have now become ethical alternatives, and allow for individual choice."(1) Educators, as well as psychologists, are moving toward agreement that the healthiest direction in dealing with the resolution of sexual problems is with open discussions and "operating permissively in the area of alternatives."(2) This has been my goal . . . to offer you more alternatives.

Sexual intimacy is one of the barometers that can be used to indicate the stability and emotional closeness of the partners. Lack of this intimate quality of sex can serve as a signal that the marriage needs attention and alteration. Sexual problems can offer a sign-post saying symbolically, "We're in trouble. Our marriage is ailing. We need help."

Frequently, couples come to see me explaining that they're not quite certain why they want therapy, "We've always thought our marriage was perfect . . . yet lately, we've started to realize that something is wrong. We don't seem to be having much fun . . . and we're both screaming at the children, all the time." As our work together continues, they become more trusting and comfortable, and are able to confide in me. We start examining the deeper, underlying problems in the marriage. It is at this point that we usually uncover the sexual problems in the relationship.

Then the couple can start their repair work and

(1) Sex Information and Council of the United States, *Sexuality and Man*, Charles Scribners Sons, New York, 1970, p. 160.
(2) Christensen, H.T. *The New Morality: Research Basis for Decision in Today's World*, Brigham Young University Studies, 8, 1967, p. 23-25.

learn to re-examine the unfulfilling and unrewarding quality of their sex life. When we are able to discuss sex more openly in therapy, we can better investigate their problems and restructure their sexual relationship.

When most couples begin therapy, I find their thinking rigid in relation to their sexual activity and problems. They seem to be stuck and set in their established sexual modes and have no alternatives. After considerable therapy work, this changes, and the rigidity diminishes. These couples become more aware of their unsatisfying sexual practices, are more willing to modify them, and introduce fresh thinking, ideas and behaviors into their sexual life. They start working with the exercises and their new adult sex information. Their healthier sexual life comes to include experimenting within the privacy of their relationship with new patterns and styles of lovemaking. More alternatives in sexual play and excitation are incorporated in their behavioral repertoires. They begin to feel better about themselves and report becoming closer and more loving to each other.

Sex is a beautiful way to share and enjoy your love. Learn to become more comfortable with the words "I WANT" between you and your partner. Hear his message, give him yours.

Getting closer to each other is such a precious way to spend your moments. Savor your sexual time together . . . it's good, it's healthy, it's normal. Enjoy. Get closer.

Chapter XVII

Throw Away Cruelty

Understanding that "we are all two-year-olds," destroys the concept of cruelty for me. I don't believe anyone is deliberately cruel. I believe we're clumsy in the way we handle our words and feelings because we're frightened and preoccupied with our own pain and inadequacy.

If someone does hurt your feelings, tell them. But when you do, try to remember how small they really are. It is difficult to understand someone is "little" and in trouble when they've just been abusive to you. Nevertheless, try to throw away the idea they've connived and plotted to assault you. I don't believe it. They aren't being cruel . . . they are insensitive, because they are so involved with their own suffering.

People feel frightened, guilty and defensive so much of the time. They are worried you're going to harm them somehow, so they strike out and attack first. Or they put their hands up emotionally and create a shield to protect themselves from the blows they expect from you. Either way, you feel pushed away and assaulted. However, their objective was PROTECTION, not cruelty.

If it is guilt that is troubling someone, they may cry out with angry and insulting kinds of communications. They may be too overwhelmed with their own sorrow to realize how their words are hurting you. They want to say, "Help me, I'm in trouble," but they don't know how. Instead, they throw out their words that feel cruel to others and prohibit help from coming towards them. They are like the small child who waves his fists in the air warding off the arms of mother who is trying to offer comfort. No one can see the attacker is in trouble, or that his negative messages are really directed to himself, and not to you. He is labeled cruel, and you, who are left feeling full of resentment, leave. You either end the relationship or "attack back."

I'd like to share what happened the other night in group. I hope it will help you understand why I throw the word cruelty out the window. This case illustrates how feelings of guilt can distort our communications.

Bea, who stutters slightly, was talking to the group about her relationship with her husband. Bea has had years of speech therapy. Although she still stutters, it is infrequent, lasts briefly and doesn't seem to trouble her.

It was getting late, and I was almost ready to terminate the session for the evening. Matt, another group member, tried to interrupt Bea's work. He spoke in a loud, obstrusive voice. Several group members shouted at Matt, telling him to be quiet. They wanted to hear what Bea was saying. Matt continued to interrupt. "I want to work before group is over," he said, sounding even more belligerent. "Bea isn't saying a damned thing worth the group's time. She's just babbling like an idiot about nothing. Just wants to be the center of attention. She's got to have the floor. I have some *important* work that I have to do."

"Matt," I said, "that isn't fair. Bea's work is just as important as yours. I want to work with you as soon as she's finished."

"I can never get a word in edgewise here," Matt continued shouting. "I don't even know why I'm in this lousy group," he said, glaring around the room. "You people are always pushing me out." Then he turned to me. "And you, Kassorla, you're *unfair* to me! Your politics stink. This is my group, too."

"You're right, Matt," I said softly. "This certainly is your group, and you're an important member. Right now I'm working with Bea." I turned towards Bea, and she continued talking about her problems with her husband.

When Bea was finished, I went back to Matt. I smiled and said, "Do you want to work now, Matt? I'd like to help you if I can; there's still time left."

Matt's face was red. "Don't give me your patronizing smile, you bitch! I'm sick of all your therapy crap!"

"You're a pain in my neck, Matt," I said. "Cut out all the negatives and attacks." His face became very pale. I could see he was in trouble. I continued softly, "I really want to help you. What's happening? You look like you're really hurting. Are you frightened about something? . . . in trouble? What is it, Matt?"

Matt's body became rigid, his face was white . . . he started crying. "I've ruined my daughter. It's all my fault; I know it. I've ruined her. When Bea started working and I heard her stutter, it reminded me of my daughter. I suddenly felt cold and stiff. I couldn't listen to Bea. All I could think of was my kid. How can I help her to stop stuttering?"

"You CAN'T! There's no way you're going to be able to help her to stop stuttering, Matt," I said. "Your guilt is in the way. With your attitude of help, you'll probably make her feel like some kind of cripple. Get out! Your daughter is lovely. Leave her alone. You've been a good father. You've really tried. Besides . . . she's a wonderful child."

Bea interrupted, "Matt, I know I stutter. But I don't do it all the time. And it doesn't even bother me. My stuttering is my *last* problem. Leave your daughter alone. If you talk a lot about her stuttering, no matter how you try to help her, she'll feel peculiar and too different. She'll be afraid to open her mouth. I'm not even aware, most of the time, when I stutter."

"Bea, I know you're trying to help me," Matt said, "but I still feel so guilty. What can I do?" he asked, as he continued crying.

"You can accept, respect and admire your daughter, Matt," I added. "She's such a sweet and remarkable young lady. She's made an excellent school adjustment . . . she adores her teachers . . . she has lovely friends and she's a talented painter. What do you want? She's doing fine. Get off her back!"

"I do respect and admire her," Matt said. "It's so easy. She's such an adorable child."

"Good," I said. "Tell her she's terrific. That's the way to help her with her stuttering——FORGET HER STUTTERING! Tell her about your respect and admiration for her. That's important! Discussing the stuttering will only serve to increase it and make her feel inadequate. FOCUS ON HER STRENGTHS. Give her your honest positives, not your parental guilt. Children thrive on positives. We all do. Stop the guilt! Besides, you're a loving and wonderful father. Your child didn't get to be that adorable without your help!"

My point in sharing Matt's work with you is that I realized something was troubling him when he verbally attacked everyone in the group. I checked with him later and he was actually unaware of how harsh he sounded. He was surprised to hear how angry he appeared to all of us.

"I had no idea I was heavy with you, Doctor," he said. "I was in so much pain—I felt so guilty about my daughter's stuttering. I wasn't even thinking about you or the group. I was just hurting out loud. I don't even remember feeling angry—just worried."

I believed Matt. I'm convinced that people who are negative or attack verbally are not aware of how they sound.

They are *not* cruel—just too covered with self-blame and pain to have the energy to pick up their two-year-old eyes and see what's happening to the person who is next to them. If you can be kind and understanding to them, they may be able to stop hurting for a while and be kinder to you. Throw away cruelty . . . behind the cruel words there is a voice filled with pain.

Chapter XVIII

Putting It All Together

Where are we going? What's the goal? Can we "put it all together?" Can we feel better about ourselves? What is the "good" life? What is a healthy person? For me, "putting it all together" is realizing that, in fact, we *can't* put it all together! This isn't possible for humans. All we can do is to try. We're all struggling with the same problems. We're all visitors here. We all have a page stamped, "The End" on our visas.

To be alive, to be human, is to feel uncertain part of the time . . to make mistakes . . . to try . . . to fail. I attended a conference in Brazil, where experts from all over the Americas gathered. The most frequent phrases I heard from my colleagues were, "I don't know" and "I'm not sure."(1) On my lecture tours, I find experts from all over the world saying, "The

(1) XIV International Congress of Psychology, Sao Paulo, Brazil, April, 1973.

more I know, the less I'm sure." Who can ever be certain? Who knows anything for sure?

To be human is to have problems, concerns, and doubts. To be mature, is to try to deal with the problems and "attempt" to work them out.

One of the goals of therapy is to develop a mature personality. But is this possible? And what is mature? If maturity embraces coming to full growth, being fully developed, coming to full excellence and being completely ready, is this possible for a human being? I think not. The human state precludes being "completely ready," "completely together" or "completely" anything else. If you're human, you're *not* complete. You're *not* perfect. And that's fine! That's what's so wonderful about being human.

The healthy person is constantly changing. He is adding to and modifying his emotional and intellectual frameworks. He is re-examining old ideas and incorporating new concepts and points of view into his reference.

I emphasized the word attempt when I suggested the mature person attempts to work out his problems successfully. I consider success to be a wedding of failure and activity, or attempting. To succeed is to keep trying and to be active. And if you are in the arena trying, you will be failing part of the time.

Patients I've treated in mental hospitals have the perfect formula for *no failure*—they become immobilized, they don't move. If you see them at 10:00 a.m., they are sitting in a chair; at noon, they are sitting; at 6:00 p.m., it is the same—they are still sitting. No challenges, no change, no risks, no activity, *but*, they have solved their problem—NO FAILURE!

Failure is a favorite area of discussion for me. I actually encourage my patients to fail! I don't think success is obtainable without a relaxed attitude toward failure.

In 1968, I conducted a motivation study in London. I interviewed and analyzed the behaviors of twenty of

Britain's "most successful men." Without exception, I found the successful men in my study had no negative emotional reactions to failure. They all considered failure to be an integral part of successful performance. When you fail, you have a clearer understanding of where *not to go* next time. That's essential information which can serve as important guide posts for your future behavior. Stop being negative when you fail. No self-blame. No self-punishment. Rather, failure means you're active; failure demonstrates you're trying! If you can fail and try again and then succeed and fail again . . . GOOD! *Give yourself a kiss.* You're on your way to success.

SUCCESS = Activity = Failure = Success.

People who are non-achievers stay home because they are frightened to try and to fail. They decide it's best for them to wait until they get over their fears. Nonsense! What they can't see is that successful people feel the same as they do—they're frightened too. But they try. They "GO" frightened. They *go* to work frightened . . . they *go* to social situations frightened . . . they *go* to meetings frightened . . . but they *go*.

It's fine to be frightened. It's human. Not attempting is what's sad, because then—you can miss it all.

And if you can get up and *go* frightened you'll be able to take a look and see what's out there for you . . . the fun, involvements, excitement, people . . . whatever you want can be available to you, if you GO frightened.

DOES EVERYONE NEED THERAPY?

I've talked about how therapy can help people to appreciate their own humanness and live more meaningful lives. Now the question arises, "Does everyone need therapy?" Getting help from a professional therapist may be an unavailable or unacceptable alternative to you. I don't believe therapy is necessary for everyone. There are other methods for developing a positive self-image, other methods for self-fulfillment and self-growth that do not require formal therapy.

One of the most important ingredients of therapy is learning to ASK FOR HELP. In our society, we are reinforced to be "do-it-yourselfers." For me, the entire concept of do-it-yourself is too limiting, too narrow in terms of utilizing available resources, and most of all, too lonely. Years ago, in the United States, neighbors used to come together to help each other build their homes and farm their fields. This working together resulted in feelings of great camaraderie, loyalty and love. I'd like to reintroduce this kind of thinking into your life. Go to your friends, family, colleagues and neighbors. Ask them for help. If you can say to someone, "I value you, you're important to me, I need your advice and help," then you will have another way to enrich the relationship and cut down on the distancing.

I've had many patients tell me that even when they are sick, they find it difficult to ask their mates or friends for help. They try to "do-it-themselves." This is sad . . . they lose a chance to get closer to their friends. The people who love you need an opportunity to show you they care. Let them. Ask for help. Let the closeness in.

When I work with successful and active patients and colleagues, I find there is very little "do-it-yourselfing" in their worlds. Rather, they have wise, loyal, loving and helping hands surrounding them. This kind of thinking suggests, "My two hands are too little, the jobs I want to do are too great and there is too little time." Our capabilities are limited and narrow. When we stand alone, and try to do it all by ourselves we *see* too little, we miss too much. If you can ask for help from friends, family, neighbors, employers and employees, research people and professional experts in your community, you can benefit from the support of their skills, information, experience and knowledge. This will increase your own feelings of safety and allow you the availability of unlimited resources.

I want to refer again to the motivation study I conducted in London with the twenty most successful British men. Their attitudes suggested that "do-it-yourself" was associated with "mediocre" performance. All of these remarkably successful men had large organizations of people closely involved with helping them. Literally dozens of hands, sometimes hundreds of hands, surrounded them with help, guiding and influencing them, taking over responsibilities, making suggestions and offering alternatives. Their equations looked like this:

Mediocre performance = "do-it-yourself" = don't get help.

Success = GET HELP.

Throw "do-it-yourself" away. Ask for help and be pleased you could ask. This is a healthy behavior.

Another way you can help yourself, without formal therapy is to *be honest*. Find friends with whom you can share your most precious secrets. You may be afraid the secrets you're hiding are too "ugly," "terrible" or "wicked" to be brought to the surface. Most of us feel our friends will leave us if they really get to know what's deep down inside of us. We're afraid they'll decide we're too "horrible" or "different" and go away. The opposite occurs. Don't hide.

When you share yourself with people, they will understand you're just as vulnerable, fragile and frightened as they are. They'll appreciate your human qualities and come closer. Tell them, "This is who I am . . . the real me. Love me, accept me."

Often when patients first come into therapy they'll say, "Doctor, I have something to tell you, but I can't yet. I'm afraid . . . it's too awful . . . something I did long ago. I'm so ashamed. I'm afraid if I . . . etc." Eventually, they do trust me and share their dreaded secrets. I usually explain that I've heard the same secret several times during that day and dozens of times the week before. They're amazed their secret wasn't horrifying and that I'm not shocked. The point I'm making is that we're all so much alike. In ten years of seeing hundreds of patients on five continents, I've yet to hear an infamous secret . . . just human secrets and behaviors we've all experienced. If you can be honest with the people in your world, you will enjoy increased feelings of self-love and self-worth.

There is another way of being honest I'd like you to consider. That is, accepting that the person talking to you, is also honest. Whatever your friends tell you—believe them. I believe everyone. This is my way. It has been my experience that people will tell the truth when they know you believe them and trust them. I do. When I was an intern, I treated adolescent patients who were classified as chronic or pathological liars. It was typically understood and predicted by the other clinicians that these young patients would lie. I believed these children. Usually after working with them in therapy for about five sessions, they'd confess to me they had lied. They would become protective of me. One of them said, "Kassorla, you're so naive. I've been lying to you for days now and you keep saying you believe me. You're so dumb it's embarrassing. Someone's got to take care of you. I guess I'd better or you'll get killed by the rest of the bums in this place. If you don't watch it, you might even lose your job. Now, listen to me Doc, here's what really happened . . . etc." By believing them, even the so-called pathological liar became honest with me. They had finally found a friend who believed them. It's like programming a computer. When you insert cards that say, "I believe you—you're honest," the computer says back to you, "I am honest, I speak the truth."

Don't look for hidden messages, clever nuances, or

covert meanings. If you want people to be honest with you, assume what they say is valid. This is the easiest and fastest route to travel.

You can imitate what happens in a good therapeutic relationship by finding peers with whom you can be honest—people whom you value, who will share their foibles and "humanness" with you, while you are sharing with them. This is how you will be able to develop meaningful relationships with open communication.

When you are honest with yourself and others, your feelings of self-esteem and dignity will flourish. You will feel valuable to you and more loving towards them.

Introducing new behaviors into your childhood package will not be easy. You can only *try*. Whether you're working in therapy, or by yourself, incorporating new behaviors into well established childhood repertoires is difficult. Expect your changing to be erratic and to occur in small steps. New behaviors become established slowly. Expect to fail frequently, and to find you are slipping back and still doing it your old way some of the time. You will probably see yourself going up and down—first the new way, then you may revert to the old style, and then back to the new behavior again, then the old way, etc.

Kiss yourself for being able to try something new, and on the occasion when you see yourself slipping back to the old behaviors, kiss yourself for SEEING and understanding what's happening. That's fine. No one does it perfectly. We all slip back occasionally. That's the human way.

There is no *instant* therapy or *instant* change. A good deal of thinking and deliberate, hard work is required. When you are learning new styles, you may experience some fear, anxiety or discomfort. This disappears if you can hang-in and encourage yourself to keep practicing and trying. Sometimes changing is frightening or emotionally painful.

You may hear your old voice trying to sabotage you by saying, "Hey, what's this changing business all about? Stop it! You'll die if you change. Your old ways may be harmful to you, self-destructive, unfulfilling, demoralizing—but at least you've stayed alive all these years. Being alive is where it's at. You've survived. Who knows what changing will mean? Maybe it will be scary . . . awful . . . disappointing . . . etc." NONSENSE! Ignore your sabotaging voice and the frightening feelings will melt away. People often suspect that changing will cause them to be less successful and creative. *The reverse is true.* Most patients report enormous increases in their creativity, thinking capacity, and general productivity. They feel more loving and appreciate the closeness and dearness of their important relationships. Above all, changing can help you to feel so much better about yourself.

GIVE YOURSELF A KISS

I started writing this last chapter in my head while I was still in bed this morning. It was 6:30 a.m. My old French prayer clock had just chimed the half hour. My house is very quiet then—it is a good time to write.

This is a special weekend for me. My house is full of love—my children are here. They're usually away at college, but this weekend they're home. Today, the walls in my house are smiling.

I went to my desk, picked up my pen . . . and I began to cry. There are so many of you out there that I've wanted to touch—to move. There is so much I've wanted to share with you. Have I done it? Have I helped you to better understand and live with your lovers, friends and children? Have you heard my words? Can you cut down the distancing now? This is important to me. Will you be able to get closer? Will you?

I've tried to help you learn to say I WANT. Now, I'd like you to hear what I want . . . I want you to be able to smile more now, to put your arms around the people you love. And even more important, I want you to put your arms around YOU. I want you to stop being negative about you. I want you to give yourself more kisses. When you have trouble changing, or when you make a mistake, I want you to say to yourself, "It's hard to change, but I'm trying . . ." I want you to give yourself a kiss and keep trying.

How can I emphasize the importance of giving yourself a kiss? What can I say that will help you to remember?

When patients talk to me about feeling stupid, guilty, foolish, crazy, etc., I correct them. "I want you to *stop* blaming yourself," I say. "You learned your 'childhood package' well. That's all you could do. You can't move out of the house when you're three. Stop saying you're stupid! You're not . . . you're just human. And you're behaving the way you were taught."

Will you hear my message? Will you hear my "I wants?"

It is difficult to help patients change their life-styles. I use everything available to me, including recipes, suggestions, new ideas, outlining alternatives, re-education, homework, marathons, private and group therapy. I also use modeling techniques with patients. They report feeling awkward and clumsy when they try out their new behaviors for the first time. "Good," I reassure them. "Babies don't leave their cribs and start right out running. They're awkward and clumsy too. First they try one step. Then they stumble and fall. It takes a good deal of practice, trial and error, before the infant can walk, and feel confident. It will be the same for you. Practice. Fall down. Get up and try again. Do your new behaviors *mechanically*, at first. Don't expect to do well. Remember when you first started driving an automobile? Remember how mechanical it was for you to learn the various steps? This will be true for your new psychological behaviors as well. Try them out. GO frightened. Make errors. Be mechanical. TRY and then, give-yourself-a-kiss."

For example, let's imagine your new behavior is delivering honest positives to your son. Your plan is to give your "garbage-can child," Andrew, some positives. Your old behavior has been to drown him in your killer messages. You think to yourself, "What can I say? That child drives me up the wall! It's difficult to think of anything positive. Oh yes, he's much neater lately about his hair. He looks better than ever since that girl moved in next door." You write down your "positive," and tape it to your make-up mirror to practice when you're alone. When Andrew comes home from school, you greet him at the door. You remember your homework and say your positives mechanically as Dr. Kassorla said to, "Hi, Andrew. My, your hair looks neat. I'm sure glad that girl moved in next door, or you'd probably still look like a mess!"

Did you try? Yes. Were your intentions good? Yes. Were you mechanical, awkward and clumsy? Yes. Was it a positive? NO!!! Calling your child a "mess" just wasn't positive! You started out fine with, "Your hair looks neat." That was new behavior. Then you flipped back into your old punishing style and added your killer message, negatively predicting he'd still look like a mess. Most patients do this at first. That's all right. It will take much more practice before you'll learn your new behavior—to be positive.

For me, you're on your way. At least, you were "half-way" positive. That's progress. If you're kind to *you*, perhaps next time you'll be even more positive to your child, and the next time even more . . . etc. You're working on change. *Give-yourself-a-kiss.*

Change occurs fastest in a supportive, rewarding climate. If you want to change, be positive with *you*, accepting of *you*, and understanding of *you*. And even that isn't enough—you need to be more loving towards you and to give yourself kisses.

I've had patients come to see me for the first time who have had five or ten years of therapy. They complain no change had occurred. Another patient who was thirty-three years old, had twenty years of therapy—still no change. Why? I believe it was this loving atmosphere of "kissing yourself" that was neglected in their therapy work.

It is possible to understand what your problem is and still not change. Often people are able to see what's happening, but they can't move beyond this first step of insight—the understanding, or *seeing*. Unfortunately, once they are able to look at the way they interact with others, they start to hit themselves verbally. They are even harder, more self-punishing and negative than they were before they could *see* the problem. They give themselves killer messags such as, "I'm an idiot! I did it again. How could I be so dumb? At this rate, I'll never change."

I'd like you to try to visualize this next example. It may help you to stop hurting you.

Everytime you are negative or verbally punishing to you, it is similar to hitting yourself over the head with an enormous hammer. With each negative blow, you knock yourself into the ground, deeper and deeper, a little at a time. "I shouldn't have done that," you say. And BANG, over the head, into the ground you go. "Why can't I do anything right?" WHAM! You've driven yourself another inch into the ground. "If only I had more brains, I wouldn't keep making these ridiculous mistakes." Ouch! Another blow over the head, and you're in, even deeper. After a while you have given *you* so many punishing messages, only your head can be seen above the ground. You're stuck deep in your negatives, and deep in the behavior you hate. You can't move. You can't change.

Stop it! *No fair*! Appreciate your struggle. Appreciate how you've tried. Appreciate your willingness to see your behaviors and to be honest with yourself. Stop hurting you!

In my philosophy of healthy behavior, you are always "giving-yourself-a-kiss." If you fail, you get a kiss for seeing how human you are, and if you succeed, you get a kiss for trying. Either way, you are kind to *you*.

Nobody *can* put it all together. But the wonderful magic of being human is hoping and trying—even when the goal seems impossible. I hope you will try. GO and find a love to share your life, friends to talk, play and cry with, meaningful work to fill your days, peers who appreciate and admire you, causes to fight for, and your own dignity and integrity to respect.

I don't know a good way to end this book. In fact the entire idea of leaving you now, is too painful. I'm not sure how. I want to avoid it. This has been a wonderful time for me—writing these words to you. I've valued the experience. I've felt good about me—being with you in this way. How do we finish? How can I leave now? How do friends say . . . GOODBYE . . .

About the Author

Dr. Irene Kassorla's revolutionary new approach to mental illness has earned her international fame as an expert in schizophrenia, autism, and family therapy. While still an undergraduate at UCLA (where she earned her B.A. and M.A. degrees in psychology) she was responsible for designing a new method for treating mentally disturbed children. Soon after she traveled the world helping mute psychotic patients to speak. In 1966 she was invited to England to duplicate her work and conduct more research. She remained in Britain 3 years and earned her Ph.D. from the University of London.

Equally famous as a television personality, Dr. Kassorla's group therapy sessions can be seen on television all over the United States. Presently she lives in Los Angeles where she is well known for her lecture and television appearances.

MORE HELPFUL BOOKS FROM WARNER...

A HANDBOOK OF YOGA FOR MODERN LIVING
by Eugene S. Rawls *(89-596, $1.95)*

Your entire family can follow the Yoga disciplines together. There are back-breaking exercises—instead, you enjoy the gentle, relaxed stretching of muscles and learn how to breathe properly. Begin to use this dynamic new approach to self-development today! The definitive guidebook to health and happiness for everyone in the entire family. Fully illustrated.

YOGA FOR BEAUTY AND HEALTH
by Eugene Rawls and Eve Diskin *(82-972, $2.25)*

Become more alive, more confident, serene and attractive—burst with energy and ambition as you follow the proved teachings of Eugene Rawls and Eve Diskin, two of America's most famous and expert Yoga instructors. Give new youth to your face and body with a modern method that is 4,000 years old! Fully illustrated with step-by-step instructions.

YOGA FOR PHYSICAL FITNESS
by Richard L. Hittleman *(91-281, $2.50)*

Enjoy vibrant good health and sparkling energy with this effective program geared for those whose work prevents them from getting enough exercise. Learn to stimulate circulation, improve muscle tone, eliminate headaches and more. Fully illustrated.

YOGA FOR PERSONAL LIVING
by Richard L. Hittleman *(91-186, $2.50)*

Ten minutes of Yoga practiced in the morning (starting out while still in bed) sets of exhilarating mental and emotional tone for the entire day. Ten minutes of Yoga before going to bed improves skin tone and hair luster, creates a suppler, healthier body, and prepared the way for deep, restful sleep. In YOGA FOR PERSONAL LIVING, Richard L. Hittleman has created a practical guide for everyone.